THE BELFAST BOY
CONTACT IED!

THE BELFAST BOY

CONTACT IED!

COLUM F. McGEOWN

Matador
9 Priory Business Park
Kibworth Beauchamp
Leicestershire LE8 0RX, UK
Tel: (+44) 116 279 2299
Fax: (+44) 116 279 2277
Email: books@troubador.co.uk
Web: www.troubador.co.uk/matador

ISBN 978 1783061 761

British Library Cataloguing in Publication Data.
A catalogue record for this book is available from the British Library.

Typeset in Calibri by Troubador Publishing Ltd
Printed and bound in the UK by TJ International, Padstow, Cornwall

Matador is an imprint of Troubador Publishing Ltd

MIX
Paper from
responsible sources
FSC
www.fsc.org   FSC® C013056

The Belfast Boy – Contact IED

The warrior never looks for it , but is always prepared . No matter how big the task . The obstacle . The objection . He will fight till the death . The warrior is passive , when the situation deems it . He is lying in sleeping . Always . When he is awoken , time stands still ...

Some of the names and descriptions of characters have been changed to protect the subjects' identity.

Preface & Acknowledgements

Army personnel become closer than family. I'm not trying to be cliché or patriotic but they really do and it's something you will never understand unless you do it. I have only come to this realization long after my army career has ended. In time and with time it can and will effect even the steeliest and toughest of mindsets. There is a deep connection to the comrades I have served with that will never die. It will remain with me till I die. I want to Thank in no particular order, Victor, AB, Chris Tobin, Bob, Al, Mo, OC, Helen, George, Greg, Mary Francis, Blair Strain, Steph Law, Pete 'The Major', The Irish Guards Welfare Team, Steve Collins and Roy Carr who convinced me to write my story.

CONTACT – IED!

We had a little brief at midnight that night. It was a fore gone conclusion. The first two months I had accepted to carry the heaviest piece of equipment in the patrol a lot of the patrols. I did this for a couple of reasons. I was older, fitter, stronger than a lot of the boys and if contacted could still move with pace. It's my nature to accept the hardest role and some of the boys can have a little whinge about carrying heavy kit , we're all human after all contrary to what the media represents . And I would do anything to avoid hearing the boys whinging. Carrying this kit I am more central within the patrol when marching. I was so conscious of IED's that I would watch where the guy in front of me put each step and I would put my feet in exactly the same footprints as I knew that these square inches of ground were IED free. I was very vigilant. As 'point man ' this luxury didn't exist but I made sure I walked on every bit of ground I was leading the men on. Our brief ended at half an hour past midnight and we were to be up at 4 ready to leave the FOB (Forward Operating Base) in darkness for 15 minutes to 5. We awoke early that morning. I barely got any rest. Semi-resting with one eye on the task ahead. The whole Battle group left the FOB leaving the chefs and other attached groups on sangers. Every man was needed as we took on this mammoth task. We left the FOB with our night vision kit on. We got held up along the way. There was so many of us. Qauds. And the ground and ground sign looks different at night through your night vision capability. The drills are slower. Eventually we all got in. Stopping and starting we all got there in the end. The PB (Patrol Base). When we were there. Remember running to the toilet. I had the runs. Bad diet. Supply to FOB. Poor. Flapping when removing new blast-proof nappy I'd just been issued. The PB was small for the whole Battle group . 20 to 40 minutes went by. Nothing to do but wait for first light. We were told to put all our night vision stuff in our daysacks. There's minutes where your standing there feeling people analysing whether or not they're in fear of what's about to happen. Hierarchy. High ranking officers. Junior G-men (Guardsmen). Senior G-men. Section commanders. I was dead jumping on the plane. Every day was a bonus. And I took each day at a time. It's a reason why I wrote a Bluey(Army Letter) to Helen every day to document everything I'd done. Felt. So there would be a written account of my life right up until the last day. It was therapy as well. If you can put a horrible. Tough. Or harrowing day on pen and paper you can cleanse yourself of it. And then start the next day as a clear slate. Moving out. First light. Leave PB. Pass HLS(Heli Landing Site). Used for Gill. First multiple(Multiple of men)long. Stretches one hundred metres. Still men to go. Going Firm. Suspense is everywhere. Trying to keep it real .Look at the vanilla sky. Feeling comes to my mind. Reminds me of the day Gill got hit. Say it out loud. Mortar Fire Control ' G '. ' Cheers mate ' . Everything said makes it clear how perturbed cus of what's slipped out of my mouth. Reassure him. ' Nah, nah, just Be careful. That's all ' . Our turn to move . We follow same bearing . 200m. Instructed to turn right. AB points to landmark. Use as bearing. Cover ground quickly. Clear as I

2

go. Fields been flooded. Poppy season. Every step sink in. Boots become heavy. Boots go in. Boots come out. Wet soil like clay. Sticks to boots. 3 times heavier. Sink half foot each step. Boys with heavy kit suffer. Moaning. Groaning. Muscle pain in the air. Hit tree line. Must cross. Momentum takes me. Chest is sore with vigilant steps over long distance. Something wrong. Startled. Compose. Advance. ***BANG!!!!***

Eagerness to get job done. 2 months earlier. Stopped. Assessed . Feels like 30ft. Most likely 10 . Or 8 . I land . Compose myself . Something different . Can't . Defragmented . From myself . No shape . Structure . An insane numbness comes over me . Hit hard . Retreat inside . Warm . Comfortable place . Feels safe . Feel nothing . Being . Washed away . What's left . Never felt before . My nose . Skull could be gone . Wouldn't know . Voices bring me comfort I am still of this world . G . OC . Chris Tobin . They're voices bring me comfort . I can't feel myself . My body vibrates . Like a bell that's just been smashed by a sledgehammer . By Quasimodo himself . Breath to breath . What just was will never be again .

ANDYTOWN

Andersonstown/Andersonstown Road – West Belfast

Troubles in Andytown

In 1988 on my road two British soldiers were lynched outside Casement Park the GAA ground. They were later driven to waste ground and shot dead. At this time and especially on this day Andytown was in a fear-fueled frenzy. It was a funeral of an IRA volunteer. The soldiers were unwittingly in the wrong place at the wrong time. They were to never of imagined the outcome. The reason Andytown was in such a frenzy. Just 3 days before Loyalist Michael Stone had attacked an IRA funeral killing three people , grenades and handgun were used. 50 were injured. He unbelievably served only 13 years of a 682-year sentencing as he was released under the Good Friday Agreement . In 2006 he was to try and assassinate Gerry Adams and Martin McGuinness at Stormont where he carried a gun and a bag full of goodies to disrupt the nomination of Ian Paisley and Martin McGuinness becoming Northern Ireland's first and deputy first ministers. He's now back inside serving 16 years.

In 1995 as a child I witnessed riots, petrol bombs going in, vehicles being hijacked and burnt to create road blocks. Soley when Lee Clegg was released from prison. A soldier. A young Para Trooper. He'd killed two joyriders. Was convicted of murder. Was sentenced. And then had the decision over turned. I even witnessed a cat being picked up, swung and flung through an army LandRover top cover, a Snatch, as it slowly patrolled past. I was expecting them to coolly open the back doors and let the cat carry on with his daily business with 8 lives left but as I would later learn this would have been classified as 'Bad Drills' so they patrolled on with pussy in the back .

I remember that day very vividly. Quite honestly it was like a scene out of *Terminator 2* , 3 choppers were out hovering all within a couple of hundred metres of each other, the noise of the engines and the rotators cut through the air and changed the wind direction on the ground. A milk crate full of petrol bombs was introduced the empties taken from a milk float courtesy of the local milkman. They were filled a third of the way up with petrol and purple and white rag was used which was lightly doused with fuel. The rags went into the bottle to the bottom or just short of the fuel and hung out the bottle top like a long 2 inch tongue ready to be lit like a fuse. The petrol bombs were strategically stacked. Not one space in the crate was empty, and they sat there like a piece of art work, somebody's creation. Somebody's masterpiece for a moment's destruction. Each rag was cut with scissors perfectly all the same size with a squared look to them and each bottle contained near exact amounts of fuel in them. Petrol bombs are a very dangerous weapon. They do nothing to armoured vehicles even though armoured vehicles become the target of many. The real danger is the effect they can have on army and PSNI personnel. They're very dangerous to personnel. They were held back until the Landrovers arrived and got within striking distance. When the bomb is lit there's no going back not only is the road watching it can explode in your hand , **POMMP!!!**. When you advance you might have to cover 70m to launch it and it might be open ground with little or no cover. The older boys would psych themselves up and then go for it. Petrol bombs are a tricky operation it can go horribly wrong for the person launching it. You leave it too late the thing goes up in your hand. Too early it doesn't have the desired effect and when it hits the target it doesn't ignite and explode. And then you bring peer pressure in to the whole equation , fucking up and making a clown of yourself . Plastic bullets can surely come your way if you're in range. The PSNI and the British army, the best police service and professional army in the world because they're tried and tested. They're proven. The Road is watching and it's very heated and unbearably intense. Every time the Landrovers came in in formation they were pebbled with petrol bombs. At night the spot lights from the choppers shone bright and hard on everything and everyone that posed trouble, I stood there 15m away from an Ulster bus as it burned, hypnotized. It was parked too close to Hoppy Dobbins a main drinking den on the Road , the front of the bar was burnt down in the process. The heat was that immense the tyres exploded like grenades and the heat torched and melted them. It was not such a feeling of us against them . More a 1984 quote, ' *If only the proles could somehow become conscious of their own strength , would have no need to conspire . They needed only to rise up and shake themselves like a horse shaking off flies* '. There was a genuine feeling of " Don't fucking attempt a thing without a battalion of men behind you – Your move " . The feeling of

6

chaos was thick and pungent. And when I say us against them , I was 11 years old and in awe of what was unfolding before my eyes. I was warned to not go near the Road that day because trouble was brewing so naturally I made a b-line straight for the Road .

The chaos-fueled atmosphere had clouded and besmirched my sense of self like a thick soot. For that night I was dirty with it. It was irresistible, charged and highly addictive, but unhealthy for the soul. I remember returning to my house that night absolutely wiped from the experience.

Matter of opinion

Myself joining the British Army coming from a predominant Roman Catholic Republican-minded community and part of West Belfast was unique from many perspectives. I was raised as I believe we all were in my area to never ring the police, The PSNI. Back then they were known as the RUC and regarded as a pro Protestant, anti - Catholic organisation. The statistics were staggering with up to 80-90 % of the RUC being Protestants. We were brought up to not acknowledge the presence of either the PSNI or the British Army.

To say that some people in my community harboured hatred towards the PSNI and British Army, Yeah that would put it mildly. I can understand my parents, people of that generation, having that bitterness in their hearts and I would even find that argument understandable. But for me to develop hatred in my heart for something that happened 15 years before I was even thought of would be an ignorant

7

stance to take. I can only be influenced by what happens in my life time. Why I would want to take that hatred and reproduce and pass it on to my off spring and keep something going that didn't even exist didn't even happen in my era is foolhardy and ridiculous.

If it was as bad as my parents' generation make it out to be then why would you want to keep something like that going. By the way my parents never did and if they did I honestly would never of listened to them but they did not trust or rely on the police service. That's a fact. All of problems were dealt with in an in-house fashion within the community from people who had a vested interest in keeping control of a trouble free community. In many ways it was like our own little wild west with our own self-appointed sheriffs.

Needless to say some people will have had an opinion or feeling about me joining the Irish Guards. My answer to that is this. For 22 and ½ years I never broke the west Belfast rules. Didn't exactly follow them but never broke them and the end result was me being broke, or, to be more generous living hand-to-mouth in the Salvation Army with half a wardrobe that came straight out of Primark. I was sporting a ginger beard with long hair, not having enough money for a descent haircut. Okay, how about I follow the West Belfast rules and live in that hostel for the next 50 years of my life and do fuck all, or break the rules, see the world, have a meaningful life, decent job, have some wonderful and challenging experiences and get paid and start a family. You obviously know what one I went for.

My childhood in Andersonstown

My childhood was quite simple I was 1 of 5 boys. It seemed to consist of playing football in the street , playing hurling and Gaelic and running a bit wild in the street.

As a young child I remember occasional day trips to lady Dixon park which was considered a fancy part of Belfast because it was a green area with large mature trees and maintained gardens . There was a good park to play in and always ice-cream vans on a the occasional warm day . Embarrassing times when my father would negotiate with the ice-cream man and try and get a poke for free . A poke is an ice cream in Belfast . There was so many of us and he worked so hard I guess he didn't want to give anyone his money if he didn't have to even if it was an ice-cream for his kids . As a young child I have vague memories of being on top of a large green hill with my two elder brothers Greg and Chris . They had bikes while I had a little blue and red tricycle . I can always remember getting to the top of this large green hill but never remember coming off it . When I took my first holy communion I chose the name Ronin . The name my mother said she was going to call my sister had she been a boy . My sister Claire Marie came after the 5 boys 5 years after my youngest brother Brendan . My grandmother Mary was still alive and she was IC (In Command) of this Royal blue cardigan that took about 3 weeks to knit . But what I do remember is having to make three vows to the priest . I think mine were , I will not kill anyone , I will not lie , I will not be cruel to animals. It's easy to laugh at the innocence of it all . When I was a child my brothers lead me to school at a very young age making sure

I could walk to and from school safely by myself . It wasn't long before I was .

My grandmother Mary lived across the way from us . She had an amazing back garden , half the size of a tennis court and prized rose bushes that she would groom and prune in all weather conditions regardless . She loved them rose bushes and because of my grandmothers age we always had work to do in her house . Her specialty was the pudding that she made every Christmas . She had a secret recipe that she wrote down purposefully before she died . She would make it in a basin that she bathed my father and all his 3 brothers and 2 sisters in . It was about 4 feet long , deep and a stained yellow throughout . Little things like this basin would have been extremely important to her .

There was a huge match being held in Casement Park which was a stone throw away from where I lived . Casement Park being where them 2 soldiers were dragged from their car on that unfortunate day . I had this money-making idea that I would stick the ladder up against the wall and charge people over . It was a good idea but guess what ' No ladder ' . I borrowed my grandmothers and I'm not exaggerating when I tell you that this ladder was probably the same age as her prized yellow basin . I got money off the first 2 people but needless to say that when all these big country boys who were up for the weekend saw that there was a free pass into Casement Park , it built momentum and I found it hard to control my own personal gate . Within minutes the stewards were on to me and I couldn't act quickly enough to jump down and run off with my grandmothers prized ladder . The ladder was about 6 ft high and had about 4 rungs on it and had clearly seen better days but right up until my grandmother passed she never stopped asking me for her ladder back . Sorry grandma the bastards refused to give me it back - my bad .

My father's house was directly across from my grandmother's and he had a concrete yard and an oily garage out the back where he could keep up to 8 cars . His name is Greg also like my eldest brother and he was a mechanic and he worked extremely hard to provide for all of us . He always smelt like Diesel and his hands were always black with oil . We were always bringing cups of tea out to him in the winter time and sometimes he would eat his dinner out in the garage . I could always feel the cold from him . He was an unbelievable worker and it wouldn't be unusual for him to be in the garage for up to 16 hours a day some days . It must have been ten years went past were he wore his overalls permanently . He got dressed up for the odd special occasion . We always had a good meal and clothes when we needed them . Having five boys two years apart hand - me - downs was inevitable and so a lot of the time you knew what your wardrobe was going to look like next year cause the one above you would be modeling it for you . There was Greg , Chris , myself , Sean , Brendan and Claire Marie .

There was rules in the house . We were told to say Please and Thank You , have manners , help each other out and do things like help the elderly with shopping and stuff . Hold doors for people . It was all a bit old school . There was a spell that lasted quite a while that nobody was allowed to talk at the dinner table . I think around this time my father

wanted to eat in peace . And there was always chores
assigned constantly . I would feel like my 2 elder brothers
felt that they were above doing anything that didn't
directly please them . On the other hand when I was asked
to do something I just did it . It felt like I was helping out
and making a difference . I enjoyed physical work . I think
some people are just made for it , to do work effortlessly .
And perhaps I was just replicating what the main man in
the house was doing . It did upset me when my elder
brother described me as my fathers ' slave ' . At times I
think he would take pleasure in invalidating me like that .
Kids can be nasty especially brothers and sisters . I could
see where he was coming from . There was always work to
be done and I always seemed to volunteer . To me work
was easy .

To be 1 of 5 boys , when your growing up you all share
one unique and common psyche . It's very unusual , like
you can exist in a very natural unthreatening way with
each other but these are the people that can and will hurt
you the most because they more or less know everything
about you up until that point in your childhood . And a
difference between 2 siblings will bring tension to the
other 3 . I sometimes felt out of place because I was stuck
right in the middle of 5 boys and because of my natural
physicality and down to the physical work I did I was the
strongest of all the boys . Albeit when my youngest
brother Brendan turned about 18 he became a beast -
strong and powerful but without my endurance and
stamina . I think that there's a tendency when 5 boys are
knocked out in quick succession all in a decade then most
of the work goes into the first 2 and they're left to more

or less school the other 3 and all 4 are left to look after the baby . I think that this is what happened with us 5 boys .

Education in West Belfast

Most of my life I've been in a male dominated environment . My primary school St John the Baptist boys school was an all boy's school even though there was a girl school in the grounds next to us we were kept separate at all times . I didn't know what a woman was really growing up except my mum , my grandma and my aunties and in a way it really shaped me . Personally I think for the better . Girls are or can be distracting and men behave differently around them . I don't know if that opinion comes from my parenting or where I'm from . Belfast can be accused of not being as liberated as other parts of the UK . It is in many ways 30 years behind . There's a political cloud that has existed over Belfast for the last 40 years . Thankfully the sun has shone through a little more with every passing year .

An all boy's school brings its own problems . And when you have 150 boys in a small space for 7 solid years there has to be a king . It's just nature somebody has to sit at the top of the pyramid when it comes to the fighting ranks , best footballer , best runner , smartest kid . I seemed to fall into the first pyramid .

Kids are cunning and a lot of the time you can get into a fight without even opening your mouth . And on a few occasions I found myself taking of my jumper and tie advancing towards

13

a crowd just outside the school gates with a shoal of people surrounding someone who out-weighed and out-reached me . On one of these occasions it was a new kid who had just came to our school . He lived alone with his mother and had just moved house; so that's why he was new , because of his sheer size or maybe because something he had said, or neither , a fight was arranged between he and I . He was already waiting for me . It was P5 . I was 10 and I remember the sticky sweat on my skin from the whole days activities in school as I took off my jumper and my tie . The goose bumps and butterfly's had kicked in as I was 50m away from the school entrance . I steadily walked towards my doom or destiny . When I looked at him I realized that he was terrified . He had dark red hair . He was fucking huge, much bigger than me . I think he tried to swing a flying knee at my head and pull my head towards it . It was a bad strategy . I swung a left hook and caught him right on the chin and the fight was over, he hit the deck , and when he got up he looked scrambled and pale . I felt sorry for him as he walked away from me to catch his bus up the road but I remember feeling elated that it was over and that I was victorious . It's bad enough getting in a fight, but the next day expect to be called in for it .

Kids just keep talking until you get done for it . So you end up standing outside the principle's office for about 2 hours the next morning with the person you were fighting with . You're made sit down when the principle decides to call you in , they usually like to keep you on eggshells for at least an hour . Then they do the worst thing: they ring your parents in front of you . The worst thing is when you hear your father on the other side of the phone and your heart drops and you know that when the 3 o clock bell goes your walking to doom not destiny . After a week the fights forgot about and then you can possibly have the privilege of observing someone else having a fight knowing that you can't get into trouble for it . That's pretty much primary school life along with learning how to read and write .

Most of my primary school years I felt I was swept along like there was something or someone protecting me . It felt safe . Maybe it was my two elder brothers or God . Like there was a chosen path which I was inextricably following . My brothers above me had both done well in there 11+ and entered St Mary's grammar college . I was not as naturally gifted academically and even after a year and a half of private tutoring at my mothers' expense I still got a D . With my tutor John I learnt quickly and really done well in a lot of the exams but then I felt safer in the comfort of his own home in a nice part of town and I had one on one training and guidance . Sitting in a classroom with 60 other pupils was an altogether different experience . So I went to De La Salle school on the Glen Road and my 2 brothers prior and my 2 brothers after attended St Mary's grammar college . 4 brothers in total went to St Mary's; I was the only one to attend La Salle .

For many years I developed a complex about that . 4 brothers attending St Mary's and Me the only one attending La Salle . We were both on the same side and stretch of road, only 200m apart, and the only thing separating us was a Bass Ireland brewery . I think they make Harp now . Whatever they made, I can never forget the smell of burning hops on my journey up the Glen Road some morning's . It was vile . It smelt like soggy out-of-date cornflakes times one hundred, and stuck in the back of your throat .

Every nation has their cuisines, and La Salle secondary school in West Belfast at lunch time is no different . The Italians have the most cuisines with pizza , lasagne and assorted pasta dishes . The French have their snails and frog legs . In India it's curry . Japan have Sushi and assorted fish dishes . The delicacy in La Salle secondary boys school at lunch time was either a Belfast bap with Bikers crisps, or a Creamy Dam . These nutritious sounding meals were available in plentiful supply from the big blue Bedford Van shop that drove up the school hill and parked in the yard in La Salle . A Belfast bap is a type of Bap that I believe is unique to Belfast bakeries . It is a domed bap the size of a coconut with hard crust on its surface top and bottom . It's cut in half, buttered, and like I said, filled with Bikers crisps . A creamy Dam is a small soft bap sliced in half lengthways; they sometimes come in a round bap or can be made up to a foot long . They come with thick processed cream with a dot of jam in the middle and covered with some type of sugary flour . *Yummy* .

One lunch time there was a fight in the school yard and someone got hit in the face with a creamy dam while the fight was in full flow . A fight in school anything is used and done to denigrate the boys fighting . I personally think the fighters should be applauded and respected for providing valuable entertainment . But because of some idiots ignorance the kid was left with nothing to do but fight for his life with cream all over his face . I'd stand back and watch the ebb and flow of the fight . The moments when the victor comes out on top and you can see the losers energy dwindle and wane when he accepts he's fighting a losing battle . At this moment I would always will the loser to come back because I know that for some people a fight is never over that quickly , that decisively and that easily . Seagulls would fly nearly 10 miles in land from the coast just to feed on the scraps left out on the school yard every lunch time . They were all over it .

My life at La Salle was pretty much the same as my life at St John the Baptist only the volume was pumped up a level or 2 . Our school consisted of truly rough kids who seemed to have no desire to learn and almost gained bragging rights to who could learn the least and be the most disruptive . With the rough kids most of them had little grey satchel bags that were tip-xed or permy penned all over . They were incredibly cheap but these kids wore these little satchels with such pride . You could fit about 8 books in it if you flat packed them and that was a tight squeeze . The grey satchels were the size of an A4 piece of paper . The lack of room wasn't important as they didn't take school that seriously and left half their books at home . On a Friday last bell they would whistle and shout their way down the hill sometimes whistling rave tunes and their voices would reverberate through everything the whole way down the hill ' *Swally Time!!* ' like they were escaping prison for the weekend . Some would bring their little trick bikes into school and I doubt they could perform any tricks on the bikes but their mates would be calling ' *Trick Nuts!!* ' which meant they would be on the front or back set of trick nuts on the way down the hill and possibly get dropped at the door . If you imagine putting all these components together that's your rough kids . The same kids would be calling for ' *LD's!!* ' every lunch and break time as they walked to their little secret smoking dens that existed within the school grounds for a puff . LD's meaning Last Draws of a cigarette .

It was an interesting mix and after a quick entry assessment there was clear divide between top middle and bottom . There was 5 classes A-E . A being the brightest I was in B . I always seemed to gel with non-threating intelligent types and in secondary school this was no different . I settled in well . The walk from house to school was long and boring and my bike was quickly introduced . To the school it was all uphill which meant the journey home was a gift on wheels . In my second year I don't even think it was a week before I was pushed of my bike coming down the hill . To add insult to injury it was a kid in the year below who did it . I grabbed him by the tie and shirt aggressively while holding my bike with the other hand and to add even bigger insult to injury he popped me two crackers on the eye and the mouth . I wanted to kill him but the steady stream of boys pushing and shoving through the channeled pathway didn't present the perfect opportunity to do so . I was seething . After that day I left my bike at home .

In and around this time my father was diagnosed with cancer and had a lump cut out of his throat and his stomach and I distinctly remember not wanting to bring any more stress to the family house that was absolutely necessary . And so fighting and getting into trouble was put on a backburner . Although some situations were unavoidable . Between the age of 12 and 18 I played Gaelic and hurling for St Johns on the Whiterock Road . St Johns GAA club is right next to the Belfast City cemetery . I loved the game for them few years . It felt like I had a real job to do and I could support the team in midfield . It was the hardest position on the pitch with the most work and running and on some occasions I played a blinder and would do well for the boys . This very physical role grasped my full focus for many a year . While playing against Rossa I had an indifference with someone from the opposing team . It just so happened that this player attended La Salle and was a year above me . I felt it had been settled on the pitch and really didn't see the drama of continuing it off it . Unfortunately I think his name was Darren had other plans .

It was my first and only major fight in La Salle and again while walking towards the Glen Road from the school grounds as I got half way down the hill and closer to the entrance there was a bit of mayhem at the entrance on the other side of the road . They were like wild bees round a hive . An old friend from primary school run past me hurriedly ' Sean .. Whats goin' on '

Sean ' There's a fight'

' Who'

'You apparently' and he ran off laughing

'Haa !..No'

And the butterfly's and goose bumps started , but it was different than before . There was more tension . I took my tie off in preparation just in case it was true . And when I hit the entrance of course it was fucking true 'No smoke without fire' and there in the middle of the bee hive he was waiting for my arrival . Now I've seen fights in school before and for whatever reason in this particular socio-economic group they think it's a very unique and interesting revelation to spit on the fighters while they're fighting . I guess it adds an interesting concept just so everyone that's involved gets a little something off there chest … Quite literally . So the lollypop man or woman assists me across the road , again , to doom or glory . And I hear Sean who just past me on the hill saying ' I missed my bus for this ' . Well thanks for that Sean but why don't you fuck off out of my face . I'm controlling my breathing now and the nerves at the same time and as I enter the bee hive I can see that he is standing square on enraged .

I instantly take a boxing stance orthodox and find out that my range, timing and accuracy are better than his . I land a jab that connects as he launches in . It keeps him off balance and I settle in 3 accurate punches later and the spitting commences . Its wild and furious from him as he's throwing his shots , I seem to slip and parry with ease but seem to be taking some shots to the head and lip that I simply can't avoid due to the lack of room to move . When I hit him an accurate shot it seems to fire him up to fire three more right at me and with all the hustle and bustle after about 4 minutes of this he seems to tire slightly . He's breathing heavy and in the middle of the fight my attention starts to go to the sound of the cars passing just 2m away as I start to tee off on his head . The fight lasted about another 6 minutes and I don't stop punching until all the anger , hostility and rage has left his body . His friends are goading and encouraging him

' Are you gona let some 2nd year do this to you ' .

His rage is blind and I'm not getting picked off at all now . But he keeps coming and after 10 minutes of fighting my friend Oran intervenes . He knows both of us and is in the same year as Darren . He breaks it up and steps between the both of us . We walk home . I can feel the lactic acid in my arms and shoulders . I feel alive and heightened by the experience . Oran says' that was some fight ' . It helps . My back is tight and my breathing is a bit sporadic .

I walk half a mile towards the POP shop on the Glen Road a little anti-climax kicks in . This ain't over . Schools bound to hear something about this . Sweet , I've got my story down . It's at this juncture that when ringing the house phone they find out about my father's cancer . Mr Muir the principle brings me into his office and explains the severity of my father's cancer and he doesn't stop until he really drives the seriousness home , I get teary eyed . The rest of my time at La Salle went awesome I kept my head down and did the best I could with what was going on in my family life and came out with a B , 4 C's and 2 D's . I

21

worked hard for them grades and am proud off what I achieved . To be honest I couldn't see myself continuing education . I was rearing to go at anything accept education .

MY UNCLES BILL AND BEN

So I left school with a couple of Gcse's and fancied a bit of bricklaying there was a huge market and demand for tradesmen at the time and I remember my mother saying ' If you have a trade you'll never be out of work ' . Her father was a brikie and so were her 2 brothers - my uncles . Bill and Ben .

My uncle Bill was early forties with red , weathered skin and pure white hair . He was a one man show in more ways than 1 . He lived in Dublin for many years and started a family when the building game went through a massive boom . At night in Dublin he would sing his stage name was Sandy Young . One Christmas he brought a piece into work , a lunch , all the rest of the boys were tucking into turkey , ham and stuffing sandwiches . Bill had beetroot sambo's . The bread was dyed pink and falling apart . Some of the boys found it hilarious . He still ate it . I called Bill white lightening for his white hair and quick wit . He was the older of the 2 uncles and he had a striking resemblance to Paul Hogan in Crocodile Dundee in appearance and personality .

Ben was my other uncle . He was well built a bit lazy on it and had white hair round the back and sides . He was bald on top with thick framed glasses . The boy's called him Ghandi . He looked nothing like him bar the bald head and the glasses .

His surname was McGaan . So it was Mahat McGaan . He would go away for hours in the car . It was rare that he did a day's work . I guess he didn't have to . He was in charge .

So the building trade seemed a natural thing to try my hand at but after a few years I quickly realized the lack of glamour . It was dirty, hard laborious work with few rewards and you worked for every penny . And from my experience sometimes you worked for no pennies at all . When the going was tough and it was on many occasions financially . The guys in the squad with the families would get paid first and the guys without families, i.e me, would have their wages cut to compensate . Regardless of how much I busted myself or done that week this would be the case . I'm all for that bearing in mind that the wife and kids actually see the money . It was a bit of a piss take when your wages would be cut for Ben because he had a family and on the Friday he would throw £60 in the fruit machine and lose it in front of you . £60 that wasn't even his to begin with most likely docked from my wages to support his family . Cheers for that Ghandi!

Around this time I was living with my grandfather who was about 68 . He was all skin and bones and still did the occasional wall . He was that good a brikie he could build a wall without a level and he was immensely strong for the size , shape and age of him . He lived on an unhealthy diet of 60 cigs , vodka , spirits , the occasional slice of bread or cheese and buckets of Tea . He was a great man . He gave me a place to live when no one else would and because of his habits I did the complete opposite and became a super fit super clean liver .

I moved in after a massive fight with my father and was never to return to the family house , it was a week before my 17th birthday . After a couple of months of working and saving in my Grandfathers' I had about £500 saved and a lot of time and freedom on my hands . I wanted a car and even though I had no licence it didn't deter me . I bought a little red Nova 1.4 that was souped up but couldn't pull your hat out of bed for £150 . It was a deathtrap . The steering was shady and when you did above 60mph the steering wheel shook uncontrollably . I didn't care it was freedom and I was making a statement . Needless to say this statement didn't go down too well with my parents , aunties or uncles who banished me from my grandfather's house . It was understandable they didn't want any drama coming to his door at that stage of his life .

TWINBROOK

Running with jackals and chancers

I left and took residence in a little 2 bedroom flat in
Twinbrook with my 2 elder cousins . They drank every
single weekend bar none and many times we would jump
on a bus and go to the Arena in Armagh and party away .
The Arena was the best nightclub in Northern Ireland ; they
always had the best music with the best DJ's and provided
the best atmosphere . Hundred's would flock to it every
weekend for escape , if only for a while . Tony , the oldest ,
worked in Bombardier - they make parts for commercial
and military aircraft - and Phil , the younger , worked as a
joiner . Tony was twenty-one and Phil was nineteen . They
were both older than me .

Tony had a reputation of being a one punch KO artist . He
was small and stocky with trimmed and fringed dark red
hair . On his face he had ginger stubble around the upper
lip , sides of his mouth and chin , like a goat . His defining
feature was his thick aggressive - looking dark red unibrow ,
which was similar in shape to a huge bat in mid flight . He
carried his chest out unnaturally far especially in front of a
crowd and on his belt he carried a little extendable baton
that flicks out in 3 stages . He carried it on his belt like a
mobile phone and he was always talking about the damage
it could do in great detail . Flicking it out and demonstrating

the leathalness of it . The one time he did need it he flicked it out and the last extendable part broke and flung off as it was flicked . He was left standing with his dick in his hand fighting a gang of 3 from down the road and he was unfortunately down the road at the time . He got filled in . The first weekend I moved in he told one such story of his punching power . He told the exact same story 12 times in one night , telling it slightly differently adding a little detail or taking a little detail away . The superlatives he used to describe his victims ' *Some big cunt , Handy cunt , Big arms , Chest , looked like a hard cunt* ' were rarely the superlatives someone who had no claim in boosting an ego or reputation would use . Describing the angles in which he landed his dynamite . Unusual angles . I know that a lot of his victims were hit with angles they had no idea about . Namely the back or side of the head . These acts of violence were neither classy or brave . I knew through the grape vine his adversaries were always hugely overmatched and not expecting violence to begin with , so were caught unawares . Tony described this approach as stealth . I would describe it as plain old bullying . If you're gona fight and prove yourself make it a dog fight or at least a 50/50 battle . What was worse was the music played in the setting in the flat when he described his amazing victories . Try listening to his repeated bullshit stories and Chris DeBurg's ' Lady in Red ' or Enrique Iglesias's 'Hero ' on repeat also (which was sung inharmoniously and loudly by himself all night). He even wore a little wooly monkey hat like Enrique did in that video . Who wears a cotton monkey hat in the front room of a warm flat in a house party ? My mind did travel to certain aspects of my life before .

Around my family house there was a huge green hedge that surrounded the property , about a metre thick and 2 ½ metres high . We lost so many footballs in that hedge . When it grew out of control we would jump from the garage roof onto it and it would cushion the fall . As a kid you could hide in it when playing hide and seek . Many summers and weekends were spent trimming it or cutting it back with secateurs . After the effort of cutting it back you had to centralize and brush the hedging and then do several runs to the dump in the car . I missed working with my dad on something like this hedge or in the yard or some other project he had going . I miss coming back to the house after a day's work and cleaning the grime of my hands much the same way he did . I wasn't copying him . We inherently understood that aspect of our own personalities . That more than anything . When we worked together that's the only time we ever felt connected and at peace with each other . That was the only time there was no bullshit or tension between he and I . He enjoyed his work and grafted hard , and when he seen me grafting effortlessly he could relate . I missed pushing my dad in a car while he jump started it or doing manual labour around the house or for my grandmother. I did miss this .

I took all my home skills with me . My job in the family house was to peel and mash the spuds . Spuds were cooked nearly every night for sometimes up to nine including my grandfather , and the house would go through a big bag that you carry on your shoulder in a week to ten days . I was good and quick at peeling , cooking and mashing , and I enjoyed the routine . On occasions when I did offer to cook for everybody in the flat completely out of my own generosity and my own pocket . Tony would make you pay for your kindness . When I was cooking a steak or sausages , he'd be standing over the frying pan breathing on your neck , not admiring the food or the way it's being cooked , but more to secure he got exactly what he wanted . The lions share . He was there solely to prevent anybody running off with what he had laid claim to . This was a fear projected from his own self image .

Tony was known to be a little shifty , especially with easy prey . Kids would ask him to go into the off licence for them if he was walking past ' *Yeah Gimme the Money , What d'you want?* ' . It was some random , innocent kid who'd saved his lunch money all week . ' Give us' two bottles of old e' and a quarter bottle of vodka ' . There'd usually be a handful of them all giving their orders and Tony would be taking the money - ' *Yeah Yeah Yeah* ' - as he listened to the orders . As soon as he got the money off them all he'd walk in and buy himself a ten glass bottle of vodzski , as he liked to call it . Walk straight past the kids he'd just ripped off , look at them and aggressively say ' **WHA!** ' as he gave them a little offensive charge . He'd then walk away with the rest of the money in his sky - rocket . If one of the kids challenged him they were usually met with a slap in the face followed by a boot in the arse , as he fought for his prize like it was American football and he was going for a touchdown . A lot of the kids just walked away broke financially and emotionally , their night ruined .

Most years around the same time the Kings Hall hosted a Dj'ing concert called ' Gods Kitchen ' , and with all the country boys who made their way into the city he'd do the same thing , sort of . After the rave:

' Yes mate I can get you anything you want . Pills . How many '.

' 50 '

' 100 quid – I need the money , come with me '

He'd lead this bloke , his victim , to a house he'd never been to before - *' Wait there , I'll be back in a minute '* - walk straight out the back , scale a couple of back gardens and come out the other side of the street with a pocket full of money , and the country boy in Belfast would be jooped , still waiting there for God Knows how long before he'd realize he'd been stung .

Doyler was Tony's best friend and around the same age as him . He had a natural ability of talking someone down while talking himself up in the same breath . As did Tony ; but Doyler made it look like an art form . Like it was natural and part of his DNA . This is how they both remained top dogs within the group . I was exempt from being subjected to this idea that they were top dogs , and they never attempted to drag me down by pushing this view of themselves upon me . They knew that my circumstances were far more extreme than theirs and that I viewed the flat as my home . My new residence . Doyler delivered stationary until he became a second hand car dealer . He was always dressed to the nineties , flashy chain and bracelet on show . He was tall and lean with a clean shaved head and face , and loved talking about himself . The reason he got a pass was because he was a character and he was a couple years older . He had a sell-snow-to-the-eskimos mentality , and admittedly a little bit of charisma can go a long way , even though every conversation was about himself , how wonderful he was and money he'd made . Doyler loved bragging about how much money he made for selling this car and that car . He had a bit of personality . He was harmless and being an only child he was a bit of a mummy's boy . His walk reminded me of the Pink Panther . He was very light on his loafers and his feet pointed at ten and two on the clock as he walked . When he walked , and even in group settings , he was always observing his surroundings , and with his dandiness and demeanour it sometimes verged on sneaky . One thing that did strike me about Doyler was his hands . His hands looked soft and manicured like a bankers . The look of someone who wouldn't know what a real days work was if it came up and bit him . Hands that had never seen a building site on a cold morning , or any type of morning . These delicate-looking hands dangled on limp wrists and on occasions he'd hold his stomach and complain of stomach ulcers , most likely the result of a bad diet . He owned a Lexus Ls . It was gold and tasty , and as he lived with his mummy he had all the home comforts , home cooked meals and his mummy picking up after him . He was never short of a few quid and used the flat purely from a house partying perspective . Within a week of knowing me he'd declared that we were best mates . It was a bit soon to be making such judgements on my behalf , but like I said I felt he was harmless and I was cool with it . I did lower to his level a little bit , putting up with the sort of behaviour I normally wouldn't . I sensed a weakness and vulnerability in him , both when it came to mental toughness and physically . I was very wrong to do this . You should never lower your values because of fear of upsetting or showing up one who hasn't got any . In time this disregard for Doyler physically and every other way would come back to me negatively .

It was good to be round him though , actually . It was good to see how the other side were living . Here's me out on my ear , one of six children . Been brought up to help those around me . Mainly my brothers . I was living hand-to-mouth in a trampy flat in Twinbrook and it was refreshing that not everyone in the group was living like that . Doyler had a life were he deprived himself of nothing . It was then I realized by looking at Doyler that it wasn't humanly possible to do for six what you can do for one . The lack of material things and financial implications are evident ; but perhaps being one of six gives you a greater concept of the things that are important in life . Gives you a deeper understanding of sharing , the human condition , because so many are living under one roof . Although this can backfire . High demand and short supply can create a very unpleasant scene indeed . But what I felt from Doyler was that it was important for him to have me as a friend even though much of the time he handled our friendship in a selfish and self serving manner . He always had centre stage , and most of what he talked was complete utter shite . It was fine . He wasn't hurting anyone . The party scenario was used to boost his own ego to get him through his working week . Doyler and Tony lived for the weekend . It was **their** oxygen .

He and Tony had their own little language . They were both carbon copies in their behaviour , language , mannerisms and attitudes . When they pulled girls , as they both did plenty of times , they had their own dialectic style when talking about that . They had little or no respect for the opposite sex , either for egotistical reasons or something more deep- routed . They talked about ' *Gimping a chick* ' or ' *Scally Waggin' a chick* ' - two of the more commonly used phrases for copping off with a young lady .

There was many others that hung around in the flat at the weekend , but Doyler and Tony were the main players , probably because they were the eldest . These two were my friends , who I would later regard as associates , and they were a jackal and a chancer . Tony was the jackal and Doyler the chancer . They're minds were always working on how to rip you off some way , emotionally or financially. They'd wait for weaknesses physically , mentally and socially and then they'd rip you apart with them . And if you fell asleep you'd mostly likely wakeup with no eye brows or patch bic-ed out of your head . A free makeover . And most likely something inserted up your back passage . A Mars bar . Hairbrush . Or some other object . Or you'd wake up with half a bottle of red sauce clunked in your underwear . All round your balls . In the party was a lot of drug taking . A lot of alcohol . Mostly blow or ectasy . In west Belfast hash is known as blow . Or it was back in the day . Not cocaine . Cocaine is a rich man's drug , although Doyler had a little bag on him sometimes . A gramme . Probably to act the big man at the party . If no one else in the party can afford coke and he's the only one with a bag , well then , in his head that might make him look like Johnny

Big Balls in front of everyone else . He'd invite a couple of people to the toilet or a seperate room to use it with him . A line or a couple of keys . A key is when you dip the tip of a yale key into the bag scoop a little pile and then snort what's on the tip of the key . I didn't like the thought of snorting anything up my nose , putting it directly to the brain . I remember the pictures in the paper of the *Eastenders* star Danniella Westbrook . With everything in full swing in the flat with drugs and alcohol Tony and Doyler would be eagle-eyed , looking for anyone who was wavering under the influence , ready to pounce on them . Everything was a big competition . If someone was feeling the effects and smacked out or about to whitey , they'd soon wish they weren't because things were gona get a whole lot worse with the attention and mind games of the ringleaders . That's the typical house party in west Belfast . Some dickhead trying to be centre stage . At any expense .

I didn't mind this behaviour or this setting : even though I was four years younger than Doyler and Tony I was never overawed . Physical work strengthens the mind , and I had tough physical discipline from my father . I could see that these two had never experienced that , and their behaviour was just a smoke screen for something they were lacking underneath . They're antics would keep you alert and sharp psychologically and socially . Observing them , I would learn to what lengths the ego will go to validate itself . Some of the scenes were very ugly , with people getting put through doors or windows , or receiving an open palm slap or worse , to keep them in check . They were associates and flat mates and the word ' trust ' is not something I would associate with any of them . I was exempt from such treatment , quietly confident even at the age of seventeen . Hardened from my childhood and parenting . One thing my father taught me was to always carry myself with pride and pronounce my words correctly . To have table manners and say please and thank you . You mix that in with a good engine for physical work and I was a little different to what was floating around .

Tony and Doyler always wore bling . In West Belfast that's a nine carat Gold chain your mother bought you for Christmas , or a bracelet , or both . They both enjoyed a whole range of Nike Air Max Classics . They did attract a special demographic of female . I don't know if this is a worldwide phenomenon but in Andytown , Twinbrook and West Belfast as a whole they're widely acknowledged as ' Hood Rats ' .

There is a term used in West Belfast for someone like this , and that is ' Smick ' . A smick will usually have a little moustache from an early age that might be twenty hairs strong on their top lip . Parading the same barcode mustache they've been growing from birth . Back in the day , Bearghaus coats , Nike air Max , and a full wardrobe of Ben Sherman shirts were all part of the Smick range . A dedicated Smick will be at the same street corner at the weekend at the same time , drinking the same carry out with the same people listening to the same rave tunes and smoking weed . Smick's are like the West Belfast version of a chav .The Urban dictionary's term for a Smick is : sum we lad hinks he is hard as nails n uses these words n phrases very often : *''liek''* n *''goin 4 a swal e nite lads''* .

Smicks and chancers are a common feature of the West Belfast and Andytown landscape . A smick is like the male version of a milly . Millies are women who used to work the flour mills . Women from a common , working class background . When Andytown did eventually start having some money spent on it . It was known as de-smickification instead of gentrification .

I embraced my time in Twinbrook as a challenge and an oppourtunity to learn , grow and hold my own . My childhood helped me in this . I knew that I had to work for everything I wanted . As a kid friends were sent away from the front door when chores were being done . Try inviting a girl into that situation , where your father has that amount of control over your day to day life . As a result girls were not on my radar , ever . I knew there was no point , and as a result of that I didn't exactly endear myself to the opposite sex .

When I first arrived in the flat there was a mountain of dirty used clothes in the kitchen . The size of this pile was huge . A two-metre high cone , with a circumference of one metre , heaped in a kitchen corner . The cone of dirty washing had solidified with time and had a dark , damp , disgusting presence . The pile and the smell of it overpowered the kitchen and emanated throughout the flat . How so many of these clothes had accumulated I had no idea , but they were there now . If there was any clothes that had been cleaned - mainly boxer shorts and socks - Tony and Phil would round them up like little squirrels storing nuts for the winter . It's something I experienced sharing with four brothers . My two eldest brothers always pulled this stunt .

Hiding clean underwear when my mother had just completed a wash . In fact I spent a lot of my teenage youth with unceremoniously aggressive underwear . Many days my underwear would be eating the arse of me . The same applied with the shower in the family house . The shower had ten to twelve minutes of hot water in the morning . Again , the two eldest used to get up half an hour before everyone else and use all the water . So it was cold showers for a good rack of years for me. If I got up early to have a shower or hid underwear for myself for a rainy day , it would of made me feel sneaky and dishonest . Don't get me wrong on a couple of occasions I did just this . But I didn't make a habit of it . It wasn't the be all and end all .

When the clothes were eventually moved after about 6 months the lilo floor was 2 different shades of brown from where the sun had bleached it and where the sun had seemingly never touched it . This brown lilo flooring ran from the kitchen to the living room . It was always sticky with drink , dirt and food . In the living room there was a three seater and two armchairs . All coloured a hidious pink . The suite looked and felt sticky and dirty . Like it could crawl out the door all by itself . You might have said to my cousins , ' *The flat's the only flat in Twinbrook where you have to wipe your feet on the way out* ' . There was no shower in the flat , and I've never been a bath man . Lying in my own dirty water never appealed to me . But Tony was . Tony would shave and have his once a week bath at the same time every Friday before he went out for the weekend . He'd shave in the bath , leave his scuzz in , leave the plug in , with his disposable Bic floating in his filth , and expect someone else to clean up after him . It would literally sit there like that until the next time *HE* wanted to use it . I took to having a ' Belfast wash ' for the duration of my time in the flat . It's basically a hot , soapy flannel all over everywhere in all the nooks and crannies , and after a week on the building site a white flannel will definitely look a funny shade of grey or black and feel gritty and rough , like the building site itself .

Phil was a lot quieter than Tony , and a lot better natured , but he was still a grot . They had the 2 large bedrooms with 2 rundown double beds . God knows how many other bodies had rested in them . I had what I can only describe as a storeroom ; a single bed was in there already and it fitted in perfectly with no room to spare . You just had enough room to squeeze through the door at night because the bed was virtually pressed against it . There was room to sit on your bed with feet resting on the floor . But you couldn't walk along side it . Unless you walked sideways . There was a small three feet wide by nine inch high slit window at the top of the cavity wall , that let light into the storeroom in the daytime , and although the electric worked there was never a bulb in the flat to put in the ceiling sockets . Some prick without fail would always break the lightbulbs at the weekend party , if they were in the ceiling . The internal doors in the flat were made of thin ply wood with egg box cardboard inside . You could put your fist through it with ease , and when someone from the party wanted to act hard they would do just that . The doors were a mess . There was punch holes in near all of them , and the walls . The flat was a dump . It was far from luxurious , and a hefty rent of £20 a week between the three of us was the going rate . Tony usually leaned on Phil and I to cover it all , as it was ' his ' flat . He's always been miserable when it comes to money . There were no other bills , as the electricity was rigged . The heating was all electric heaters , and part of the rigged electric .

Twinbrook is one of the rougher parts of West Belfast that attracts large socio-economic problems such as joyriding and vigilante parties , and provides homes for a lot of people who rely on benefits . The housing is in the cheaper end of the market because of its location and surrounding environment .

The kids in the surrounding dwellings proceeded to brick our windows when they felt like it - and when I say kids I'm talking three - to seven – year - olds . They left the kitchen window with barely any glass attached to the frame and three or four stone - sized holes through it . They were unruly , and being dragged up through childhood . They would wrap on our door looking money , and the language that came out of their mouths was shocking and disgraceful and of a violent and sexual nature . Their parents were not doing a good job , and I didn't envy what I imagined these kids would one day become . I once came back from the town to see something burning on the field outside the flat . Yeah , you guessed it . It was my car . About twelve kids between the age of three and nine had pushed my car into a field and set light to it . I wouldn't of believed it had I not seen it for myself . We would watch them tip black bags of rubbish onto the patch of grass at the back of the flat , the back garden , then wrap our door and offer to clean up the mess they'd just created for a pound .

Doyler heard of my car-less predicament and offered to get me a new car , as I had a couple of hundred quid sitting about me . He gave me a list of seven or eight cars and told me to choose . He wanted the money up front without me seeing the car . ' Nah ! You're alrite mate ' . I picked up an AutoTrader and the list he gave me came straight out of the bargain buys , the exact same cars on his list , the only difference was the extra hundred quid he had on each of the vehicles . Must have been Doyler's personal delivery charge . If I was buying a car I'd be looking a couple of quid knocked *off* the asking price . Anyway , only a fool hands over a couple of hundred quid on blind faith to someone who was , at the time , a stranger . God loves a trier , though I kept my money in my pocket .

One of my first occasions out with the boys in Twinbrook , an incident occurred that came back to bite not everyone that was involved but the flat . We were in Becketts bar . I was getting to know the group . Becketts was the local for us . Some of the group had a sleight-of-hand problem when it came to women's handbags , phones , or unguarded drinks . On the way home that night , some random bloke threw a glass bottle at us . It was a bad move . For him . I was the first to backtrack and start landing shots into his head . For all I knew I was the first and only one to go after him until another five or six piled in to give him a kicking . I was with my cousins' group , which I seemed to be getting swept along with because I was living with them in the flat . I wasn't pleased . There was no honour in it . And it displeased me even more to hear some of the group laughing and bragging about the whole thing . It didn't sit easy with me . I could not return to my parents' house . Or my grandfather's . I was stuck in this flat with my two cousins with their group of friends , and I seemed to be getting involved in bullshitty situations with the group that I felt I could handle by myself . Around that time I felt powerless . I had to go with the flow .

Two years of my life went past as I would live my life in Twinbrook although not always with my two cousins . I lived with my uncle for over a year also . I'll speak about that later . The money I had saved in my grandfathers' quickly went , and the partying to the Arena in Armagh every weekend slowed down and eventually stopped . I wasn't looking after myself and I was eating the wrong foods , cheap foods that lacked the proper nutrients needed to keep me in tip top shape . Chinese and fast food was on the menu frequently . The problem was that my two cousins never really took living in the flat too seriously because they could run back to their mothers' and their fathers' houses anytime they liked . They used the flat mainly for a drinking den . But for me it was my home . Pitiful , I know . But true . I got frustrated , and then I would clean the flat spotless , only for it to look it had before I cleaned it , a few hours later . Beer tins everywhere , and beer and wkd spilled all over the floor . Cigarette butts and used joints overflowing some random bowl or saucer or cup that would need to be cleaned and reused because there was a shortage . The flat was horrible . And the reason it was horrible is because my cousins were horrible . They had no respect for the flat or anything in it .

After a few months the incident with the bloke outside Becketts who threw a bottle and took a kicking came back to bite us . The fella that got lynched was obviously a local from the community and collared where we were all living . One Saturday morning after the night before , our side door was kicked in and two men stormed in with hurls . Hurling sticks . At first no one knew what the fuck was going on . Then it became apparent . There was women in the flat . My two cousins' girlfriend's . And when I say came in , I mean came in swinging . They were roaring profanities about what had happened outside Becketts . We locked ourselves and the girls in the two back bedrooms and held the doors closed tight . The men proceeded to smash the place up . My Tv/Vhs player combo took the hit , along with doors and any other breakables . There was nothing in the flat of any value anyway . Except my Tv . Within an hour the girls had packed their stuff ready to go to their respective homes , and the boys weren't long to follow . Tony went to his fathers' . Phil went to his mothers' . Leaving me alone .

The door had been kicked in and a kitten could have rested a paw on it and it would have opened . My home was this stinking , £20 a week flat that had been targeted by some angry locals out for revenge . And I was here alone with a door that a strong wind could open . I didn't want to stick anything against the door to jam it . I thought that would arouse suspicion that somebody was in . So I left it .

I had a brick that I would flip and toss and turn in my hand to get used to it when I was building a wall with one faced brick . I thought I could just bash them over the head with it when they came back . Then I thought , Nah , bricks are heavy , and what if there's more than one . So I set up elaborate sharp items at every room in easy-to-get-to places . Under cushions . Behind furniture . Light , sharp objects such as knives , forks , pens and a handsaw from Phil's tool bag , that could inflict pain and severe damage to deter them when they advanced through the flat again . Forks that I could puncture their throats , eyes or temples with or damage them if worst came to worst . Easy to get to innocuous objects . The element of surprise and brute force . Strength and aggression would be essential .

I paced around between the living room and the hall way waiting , just waiting , with my heart rate kept low and steady . Ready to erupt with an explosive surge . If and when . I couldn't sit or rest . I stayed away from the kitchen . A back alley ran parallel to the kitchen window and they would clearly look in before entering again . I didn't want to give anything away . At about 6 in the evening I felt an energy outside the front of the flat . I heard voices and seen movement .

The front door is to the side of the building . It was the only way in and out . There were two storeys , and the concrete stairs leading to the upstairs flat provided protection at our door . You wouldn't know if the door was open or not until you were right next to it . On the other hand if you'd come in from the back you have ample time to plan an attack and see what's coming because you had a clear view of the door and the kitchen window . As you look out the front living room window you'd see the concrete path . It led to our flat and other flats . It's just to the left of the living room window , followed by a couple of concrete steps that lead down to quite a large parking area , a quarter the size of a football pitch . Beyond that was a field with one set of goalposts that's seen better days . That's the field that my car was pushed onto and burnt .

A small contingent that had gathered just five or six meters from the flat , at the bottom of the steps to the front . This had never happened before . It was clear what was happening . They had their carry-outs and were comfortable , both morale - wise and being wrapped up in hoddies , baseball caps , scarves and Berghaus coats . Some wearing beanies to keep their heads warm .They were laughing and joking and talking loudly . I was ready , and it became very real . My heart jumped a beat . My back grew tense , even tight . I stayed in the living room . I was waiting for the door to be kicked in again .

I methodically clenched my hands pumping blood to my biceps , triceps and shoulders . Preparing arms, hands and shoulders for lethal capability . The tension lasted half an hour but nothing happened . I observed that they looked relaxed in their legs and not tight and ready for action . Maybe they observed Tony , Phil and their two girlfriends leaving and thought the flat was empty . They were wrong , I was here , pumped ready to inflict pain when they entered . There was around eight of them talking laughing and giving off an aire of dominance and victory . Marking their territory with small talk , posturing , and loud rave music that wouldn't be out of place in the Arena , Armagh . They weren't moving . I couldn't relax.

I quickly realized they were there for the night , and after about five hours of pure anxiety , when it got dark around about eleven , I slipped out the side door and into the darkness . I think one of them noticed me go as they had taken residence in the middle of the path . Ten metres away from the front door . I stormed off quickly , quietly and with little trace . When I got 200m away in this profile through a series of dark twisty streets and route's I hadn't taken before , I stuck the boot down and opened up a good 800m sprint towards Dunmurry golf course in case they had quickly twigged what had happened and a chasing ensued . They didn't follow , not to the best of my knowledge anyway , and as I got further and further away from the flat I felt free and relieved . A pack of hyena's can take down a lion . Sometimes the lion has to retreat to fight another day . As I walked towards the golf course I saw a fox with a white tipped tail . I had seen this same fox many times before . This time I felt more connected to him than usual . Two survivors doing what they must . The first time I ever saw him I was in awe of him . How such a beautiful animal could exist in such treacherous circumstances . I was quickly understanding . I cut through the golf course to get to and from Twinbrook and Andytown . I would always make my way to Blacks Road and cut through Dunmurry Golf Course . Hop over the gate . And make good time . I advanced towards Andytown . The only place I could think of for a bit of solace . My grandfather's . So I went for it .

It's about a mile and a half out of Twinbrook through council estates and a series of back alleys , towards Dunmurry golf course , which is about a mile long as the crow flies . When I say golf course , don't get no bright ideas . It's about the only golf course I know of in West Belfast . It's not that big and a lot of the blokes that use it bunk on when the owner's not around for a couple of free holes . Some of the holes you need to play twice to make up the game ; there's only nine holes and another hole goes from a separate piece of land onto the main course with a main road running through it . It's dangerous to say the least . When the owner or his sons are out in the quads you usually have to take a right flank on the course , which adds two miles instead of one . It's all open from the Twinbrook end . Once you go through the course you come to a large stone wall and heavy gate . It's just as simple as hopping up and over . They always stuck grease on the top of the wall so naturally I used the gate . It was easy . On to the Blacks Road and down Ladybrook hill . Once I'm at the bottom of Ladybrook hill the entrance for Riverdale is just adjacent to the entrance for Ladybrook , and about half a mile into that estate my grandfathers' house beckons .

I rocked up outside his house ; it was close to midnight and the street was quiet and dark . The occasional taxi I heard approaching in the distance , slowing down and speeding up over the speed bumps , closing in on where I was standing . Riverdale being a little estate owned by a bunch of wealthy solicitors . A lot of them are DHSS rentals also . About a thousand houses in all . I knew my grandfather wasn't back because the curtains had not been pulled and I could see that his box of cigarettes and lighter were not sitting on the fireplace through the window . I was on but I needed to hurry because any one of these Taxi's approaching could be his and I was still banished from the house . His next door neighbour Sadie was the last of a four house dwelling block . I jumped her fence like a ninja , without bending her flowered shaped iron gate . It was at least two metres high and I eased myself down so as to not wake her . I was quiet as a mouse . When I was in her back it was plain sailing . A gate opened between her house and my grandfathers . If my luck was in , the back door would be open , or , worst case scenario , one of the windows . I was in luck . As I opened the back door I heard the key go in the front door , it was my grandfather . My timing couldn't have been any better . As my grandfather was talking , paying the taxi driver who'd helped him to the door , I gently eased the door closed focusing on pulling the handle down so the lock wouldn't click . As my grandfather went to his right towards the living room , I snuck round to my right , waited till he'd closed the living room door , and then made my way upstairs placing my feet on the sides of each stair as I advanced , to alleviate creeks and noises , before easing myself into the spare room , where I could get some rest .

My grandfather had been drinking , and this helped nullify my presence . I woke up the next morning and knew it was Sunday as I heard the front door open and my Aunty Janet shout up to her father , ' You alright pop ? , Wake up , rise and shine ' . It took a while for my grandfather to rise , but eventually he did and went straight downstairs , were my Aunty got him ready with a cup of tea and filled him in with what had been going on in the world of Janet and her kids the past week . I heard them talk for about forty minutes before leaving . Every Sunday she takes him to the Park Centre for a fish supper and it usually takes a couple of hours of his Sunday . They left and I relaxed . I went downstairs and straight into the kitchen , which was at the back of the house - my aunties and uncles have been known to drive past , and them seeing me through either of the two front windows would not of been good for me . They were all in agreement that I had been irresponsible and should not be allowed near my grandfather's , especially without him there .

Poverty is an issue in and around Belfast . Community , and especially families , come together under oppression , and a strong family network compensates for any deficiencies . Whatever one says , the others all agree . They would of marched me out the front door had they known . I opened a tin of beans , cooked and ate most of them , and tried to leave the kitchen exactly the way it was .

A tin of beans never tasted so good . I left the house at about five to time my arrival at the flat for about half six . I thought that might be a safe time to rock up to the flat . Thinking logically , if anything was going to happen they weren't going to have their Sunday Tea and then come out for a war or a bit of madness . I advanced towards the flat and had the impression that everything that had went before had settled down . I could feel it in the air .

I was genuinely expecting to come back and see the flat in flames , but the worst that had happened was the door was open , and the kids or the wind could have done that . It was a couple of days later that my cousins returned . Along with the electricity being rigged , the owner or lodger before had started a little catalogue book scam were they would order CD's to the address and not pay for them . A CD was there and it had been sitting on top of the pile of mail that had come through the door . The mail and a CD was addressed to people I'd never even heard of . The CD was Moby , *Play* . It was incredible . A complete contrast to oppressive grey , bleak Belfast . It was invigorating , colourful and soul-lifting . A gift directly from God . And to this day I still have a deep connection to that CD .

When my cousins returned . Both of them looked well-rested , well-fed , clean and healthy . For a couple of days before they came back it felt like the flat was mine and I imagined what it would be like one day to have a place that was nice and comfortable , where I could come home from a job that I loved doing , a job that I was good at , and have a Steak dinner and a glass of red wine . I wasn't even a big drinker . I didn't even drink wine but I was in love with the idea of it all . The first thing Tony did when he entered the flat was smile and shake his head in disbelief at me staying there after the door had been kicked in . But I had no other option . After that , in the next few days he and Phil went through the motions of letting me know who was where in the pecking order . It's what I experienced throughout my life being the middle of five boys and having older cousins . They think age is a pre- requisite for alpha status or male dominance within a group . I never bought that . I couldn't afford to . I was middle of the pack , but bravery , honesty and character were the pre—requisites for my model of alpha status and I lacked nothing in those areas . It was embarrassing and ridiculous . They get spooked run back to their parents . I stay . Strategize and plan the worst possible outcome against eight , and possibly kill , or get killed or severely injured . And in their minds they're both more alpha than me . They chose *NEVER* to talk about that situation *EVER* again . I don't blame them , their balls dropped and they ran off to mum and dad . Admittedly , I had my little one night stay in my grandfather's , but came back the next day .

I was coming to the realization that nothing was what it seemed . Life in Twinbrook was hard and challenging , what with working on a building site all week only to come home and rest my head in my little one-man bedroom-storeroom . The window never even opened , and when anyone ever asked me where I slept I'd always say , ' *That shoe box in there* ' . That's what it felt like , and never did I look out that little slither of window . Not once . When you find yourself living in that sort of predicament you never look outside . You look within and hope for better days . It was challenging having all these strangers in the flat that I had no control over every weekend . The noise , the partying , the constant bullshit that comes with that . The big ego's that drifted in and out of the flat like it was a dump and fit for one thing , a party . The lack of privacy that would last over a year . It was all a mental challenge . I was going through change . A change so permanent to my psyche that I was being drawn to a place that I would never come back from . There was no coming back . No unscrambling or unbaking of what I was becoming , no changing the direction I was moving . I wasn't just stepping into the unknown . I wanted to . Never have I been happier or felt more myself when I'm doing the unimaginable , the unthinkable . I was seventeen or just turned eighteen and my GAA career was over . St Johns GAA club was over five miles away , and , my car being burnt , I didn't have it in me to walk the five miles and train an intense session two or two and half hours , then walk back to an empty fridge and get up and do a day's work on site . I was living day to day . Survival took precedence in my life .

All my energy was focused on survival . Nothing more . And with working every dry day I could on site , there was simply no time for a recovery period . It was Work . Eat . Survive . Sleep . Wake up and repeat .

On a job one day we got the news the Twin Towers had been hit . We were all on a massive retaining wall out in the country . The wall was about a hundred metres long . It was tall , and with an unusual bond in it . Myself and Paddy Brown , the labourer , shoveled the mortar from the tubs straight onto the wall . Bill and Ben spread the muck on the wall and then we hand balled the blocks from the bales straight on the wall . Bill and Ben tapped and pushed them into place . With everyone grafting and pulling their weight the wall went up quickly . Initially we used a block called Farmers' Friends , which is two standard blocks stuck together as one .

Ivor , the guy we were doing the job for , came out . ' One of the Twin Towers has been hit by a plane . It's burning and people are jumping out of it to their death . ' Forty-five minutes later he came out again ' Another commercial flight has crashed into the other Tower . It must be the Saudi's . '

It was a truly amazing spectacle . Nothing felt the same after that day for a long time . It flooded the media . If New York city . America . This super power can be attacked so symbolically . So ruthlessly . Who's safe ? .

The effects of 9/11 were to shape my life 10 years later . Although I couldn't watch the footage at the time , the flat didn't have an aerial feed from the roof . I resorted to using a metal coat hanger and turning it into a quadrilateral . I used phone books and tapes along with the wall to hold in the aerial in the feed hole . But after a while the aerial feed hole was so wide that the hanger just slipped out . My combo became unusable for terrestrial Tv and was fit for only one thing . Vhs tapes .

It wasn't long afterwards that our time was up in the flat . The guy that owned it had just had a little girl and the flats were getting all new windows , heating systems and cleaned up by the council . It was a no-brainer . He wanted us out and he wanted his flat back for him and his new , young family . My time in the flat lasted just over a year .

UNCLE PACKIE

About 2 months before this happened my uncle Packie had moved in about 500m away in a block of flats . They were massive , unpretty and ugly to look at . However . Were nice and neat and cosy inside . This description applied to my uncle Packie as well who many thought resembled sloth out of the movie goonies . This was unfair to sloth . However in many ways my uncle Packie had a heart of gold . One of my first encounters of my uncle Packie in Twinbrook was the first night I moved in . I'd just been banished from my grandfathers' . His fathers . I saw a car creep up and stop by my Nova at early hours in the morning . I thought it was the hoods trying to steal my car . I quickly put on a pair of trainers and ran outside with a hammer in my hand . It must of been half 2 in the morning and I was outside with my trainers , jeans with no shirt on and a hammer in my right hand . I was standing there as the car pulled away from the parking area at the front of the flat . It stopped and came back when he'd seen me . I then realized that my uncle Packie was doing a quick recce for my parents and the rest of the family to see where I ended up .

So my uncle Packie gave me his back room . It was cosy and warm and the bed was much nicer and the bedroom much bigger than what I had been living in for the past year . There was a single bed pushed into the far corner of the room . The room had a medium sized window and an old sock drawer were I could store socks and clothes . The carpet was industrial style blue and looked thin with age . I knew that it was going to be much quieter . My uncle Packie wouldn't have any toe-rags in drinking and ruining his flat . I was about 18 and 1/2 and used this extra room and set-up to get as physically fighting fit as I possibly could . He had cable Tv but just the basic package . He got Eurosport on that package . One day I was watching the boxing . I hadn't watched boxing in so long but always loved the Great British fighters Benn , Eubank , Naz , Collins and of course Tyson , who isn't British . But one day when watching I seen this fight between Sugar Shane Mosely v Adrian Stone . It had an incredible Ko . The way Shane Mosely swung and hooked and missed . He even looked beautiful when he missed . I thought he was amazing with his speed and power and accuracy before knocking him out cold . It was artistic savagery and after watching that it inspired and drove me to be the best I could possibly be from a physically fighting point of view . It was easy I had all the time , focus and energy and most important - space to do what I wanted . I was still getting the occasional day with my uncles . There was a lot of work on and some weeks I would get a good wage . The work was good . Filling skips , labouring to the brikies , digging founds .

The work was good and so was the money and I was eating , looking and feeling a lot better and stronger . But as Packie was the older brother of the 2 uncles I was working for , all it took was a simple phone call to know what I was getting paid and it quickly became apparent that there was a different side to Packie . A greedy , self-indulgent , controlling side that didn't sit easy with me . He joked about the money you were going to give him . But it wasn't in a haha way . It was in a *if you don't give it to me you'll be out on your ear because you're living in my flat way* . I didn't like him knowing my business many times he had your wages spent on stuff to do with him or his flat before you even earned or received it . At times he was very precise , assertive and aggressive about what he wanted and when . And at one point I remember saying ' Packie , I don't know what you want , but I don't have it ' in a pissed off tone . Things settled down after a couple of months and I guess certain boundaries had been established .

I also watched the series *The Deadliest Catch* . On UkLiving , I think . I wanted to be on them boats with those boys for them 2 months in them seas . Fighting the ocean . Reeling in them cages of crabs . Walking away after 2 months with $30,000 US dollars . But Dutch harbour was a long way from Twinbrook and I knew it . It looked exciting and dangerous and challenging . I kept this to myself .

I was working and earning and most importantly I was happy and warm inside . There was some routine , freedom and stability . At night I would close my bedroom door stick on a cassette tape on my little cd player and shadow box and train for no less than 2 hours every night . I got a better night sleep when I did this and I was getting on well with Packie . Packie would work the door , taxi or deliver chinese . The taxi regulations were tightening up around that time and new and improved regulations that reduced pirate taxiing reduced Packie's earning power to the door , and delivering food a couple of nights per week . I seen my uncle Packie doing a bit of damage with some birds that he picked up on the door . It fucking blew my mind . The spell I lived with him he enjoyed a healthy supply of kebabs and chinese . God wasn't kind to Packie he had white receding hairline which was bald at the top and started loosing his teeth at a young age . He drunk buckets of tea like my grandfather and he smoked about 30-40 a day . He was late 40's and genuinely was a mix between doc from *Back to the Future* and sloth from the *Gonnies* and his weight fluxuated between looking 6 months pregnant to 9 months pregnant . Back and forth . He was between 18-20 stone . Many nights he would fall asleep listening to *Westlife* blurring from his room . I recently discovered Mike Tyson loves *Westlife* so no shame there Packie . Me on the other hand . *Westlife* represented pure Irish Cheese with their pop idol looks , gelled hair and angelic voices . Despite all that he could still get his way with the women get them into his bed and get his rocks off .

The morning after he'd sometimes quiz me , ' *What you think of her* ' .

' She's alright Packie – Sweet ' , I'd compliment trying to be neutral

He'd give me a big gummy smile

' *Get them aye ye'* , *Let big uncle Packie in Ye!!* , *Ya dir-dee Bitch Ye* ' he'd say in an animated and self assured way in his nasally high pitched West Belfast accent

He'd turn and grab his keys on the way out the door and go and do his messages in the car .

One chick he brought back her name was Hope . She was late 30's . When Packie introduced me to her I thought she was quite attractive and thin and I liked the way her hair was done . It looked like a natural perm and it was jet black . The pants she wore made her bum look perked and tight . She couldn't have been 7 and 1/2 8 stone . She was quirky with me in front of Packie . I thought nothing of it . She was Packie's girl - out of bounds . But over the coming weeks she became increasingly interested in me . They were sharing a bed but there was no sex going on . She was playing hard to get and teasing a lot , I could see by the way Packie was carrying on . He wasn't walking around like the big ride . He was smitten waiting and hoping for his day to come . One morning she openly made her way into my room and started blowing on my back as I lay in bed . It felt good . My shoulders had been burning from the workout the night before .

Packie ' *what are you's 2 doing in there* '

Hope ' Nothing , what are you shouting about '

Packie ' *Coco* (what my family used to call me when I was younger) , *What are you's doin* '

Me ' Nothing mate - just talking '

At that I waved her out she knew what she was doing . I did feel turned on by the whole experience . It was the first time that somebody . A woman . Had come into my room where I was sleeping and made it clear that she wanted to fuck me .

To be honest women or a woman was the last thing on my mind . I was fit and strong and focused and didn't want to waste my energy on some random woman . Only after 3 weeks of Hope and Packie knowing each other Packie proposed to her and she knocked him back . It was clear Packie was clutching at straws just to get his hole . Fucking proposing and everything . Nutcase . We were all in a bar one night playing pool Packie , Hope , myself and my cousins Tony and Phil . A big crowd of us . It was clear they weren't getting on and when Packie said ' *Come on lets go , we're going* ' . Hope was like , ' Fuck off I'm staying here with Coco and the boys ' . Packie was furious and stormed out .

We continued on playing pool and having drinks . Then Hope had a bright idea as the night went on ' Lets go back to my place and smoke some dope ' . I wasn't a smoker but it sounded Ok to me . My cousin Tony and his friend OB joined us . Hope's flat mate and best friend Holly was there as well . We all shared a black Taxi over to the other side of town . In the back of the black taxi Tony , OB and Holly jumped in first . Hope and I jumped in last . We ended up facing each other . She wouldn't take her eyes of me and slipped her shoe off . Put her small foot right between my legs and started expertly playing with my balls and dick with her foot and toes . It was a bit too much . After a minute I poised up controlling my urges , ' And what about Packie ? ' in a what do you think you're doing tone of voice

Hope , ' I don't want Packie - I want you Coco '

Believe me right up until that point in my life I had deprived myself of them urges . I wasn't were I wanted to be physically , mentally , emotionally or financially and so I didn't indulge in distractions . I didn't want to bring a child into this place that I found so confusing . So joyless . So lifeless . My unconditional love for a child would lock me into Belfast and I would never leave . This fear literally kept me celibate . My fear overpowered my desire at least 10 to 1 . I thought to myself where is this going to take me . Hope had depth . There was vulnerability in her being a former heroin addict and working girl . I wanted to hold and protect her and give her the love that I was . The love that she wanted . If only for a while . We smoked dope and then I got a taxi to Packie's . I couldn't do that to him - bite the hand that fed me . It would of broke his heart and he was putting a roof over my head . I entered the flat the next morning , ' You should stay away from that Hope , She's no rules at all '

Packie , ' *I know* '

Making it clear that nothing had happened and that I was with him , ' I'm serious you should stay away from her – she's fucking mad '

Packie , ' *I know Coco* ' , He was lying in bed with the door open and sounded vexed this time

Me , ' I'm away to bed ' , I was wasted it was about 6 in the morning .

ANDYTOWN - THE PRODIGAL SON RETURNS

It wasn't too long before my little era with Packie was over .
That ugly big block of flats was getting knocked down and
everyone in them was getting re-accommadated . After our
little Hope affair and living with each other for about a year
it was fair to say that Packie wanted to move into his new
place alone . He was more than happy to get me out of his
skin and recommend that I had matured over the last
couple of years and might once again be fit to return with
my grandfather as I was a new and improved version of my
former self . *Cheers Uncle Packie !* And so I did . I moved
back in with my grandfather and I was new and improved .
As I was now back in my grandfathers' I had the time to
think and plan . My grandfathers' house was absolutely not
being used as a partying den . I didn't have my Uncle Packie
around . My grandfathers a nice , quiet man who keeps
himself to himself and this made it easier to separate
myself from the pack and go for what I really wanted . The
last 2 and 1/2 years of struggle and challenges had held me
in good stead and I looked and felt different . More
importantly I looked at the world differently . I was like Neo
from the *Matrix* when he refuses to be controlled by the
system . I had an inner resolve that was always there but up
until that 2 and 1/2 years of my life it had not been proven .
I had proved something deep inside myself . I knew that I
was to get out of Andytown . My mindset was too big and
colourful for it . I was a dreamer . In and around this time I

discovered self -help gurus like Anthony Robbins who said things like *' Don't overestimate what you can do in a year and don't underestimate what you can do in ten '* . Dr Wayne Dyer . I read books like ' Think and grow rich ' . The book ' The Alchemist ' blew my fucking mind - talk about escape . I immersed myself in Confucius . Analects that are as hugely vital today than over 2000 years ago when they were first quoted . I was hungry for knowledge . Answers . Challenges . Anything that would take me out of this place and bring me to a better life . A life that I deserved . A life that I wanted . A life that I desired . I was pumped and ready for anything .

The Road is the stage . When you walk the Andytown Road you're on display . All your weaknesses . All your strengths . The feeling on the Road is tense with a lane of traffic going up the Road and a lane of traffic going down into the Town . As you leave Riverdale . My Grandfathers' estate to hit the Andytown Road . Connolly House the Sein Fein advice centre is 40m away and sits at 11 o clock . Within a 200m radius you have everything that you could ever want from cradle to the grave . There's chineses . Bakeries . Butchers . A petrol station . Cafes . Bars . Chippys . An ice cream parlour . 4 different banks . 3 different chemists . A couple of dentists . An opticians . An undertaker . A church which faces Riverdale entrance . The entrance I leave every day to enter the Road . You have the entrance to Casement Park 200m away at 3 o clock as you leave Riverdale . Before that you have Andersonstown Lesiure Centre were I spent many childhood summers at the summer scheme where I learned to swim by a guy named Brendan . A famous Blues singer by the name of Rab McCullough taught me how to dive correctly . He blossomed very late as an artist but when I was a kid he was one of the guys who patrolled the pool . A Life Guard essentially . A great guy and a real gentleman .

In the men's changing room for the swimming area there's 4 warm showers and 1 cold at the end . These showers in these changing rooms after a swim above all else represent who the big players are and who's where in the food chain . Around these showers can be as complex as any ecosystem . Any food chain . The showers in Andytown lesiure centre to me is where I could have a prolonged warm shower with no one bothering me . At off peak times . Parents not whinging at you . Believe it or not I got more privacy in Andytown lesiure centre than I did in the family house with all my brothers running around . But like I said before , there's politics around these 4 warm showers and the cold one . The cold one can be used by the much older boys to dunk and hold a young cheeky kid under to teach them a lesson . I might've been held under this shower myself once . It can either be a much older boy trying to look like the big man in front of his mates or a couple of boys your own age who gang up on you . I've always enjoyed a cold shower . Treated it like a bit of a challenge . And it's better for you . The main politics came in the shape of fully fledged men coming over while you're having your shower and checking the temperature of the shower while you're in it . This symbolises a couple of things . They want the shower you're standing in and you have 2 decisions . Walk away and leave your shower or you'll be coolly and effortlessly nudged out . And 2 . They test the shower by raising their arm like they're changing a light bulb which as a kid shows you that they're taller than you and you usually have a good view of their hairy armpit which expresses massive disrespect to the kid in it . The day you can look sternly at the older ones from boldly trying it on is the day you step into another realm in the shower area . You step into manhood .

When we were kids the main greasy spoon on the road was called the Coffee House . On a Saturday my mother would sometimes bring us here for a fry . It was considered a treat . The Coffee House had the best sausage , bacon , egg , soda and potato bread going . On the weekends they did great business . Especially on the weekends . It was cheap and the gear was good so this made it a hit on the road . If you were eating-in the food would arrive with a little side salad . A leaf or two of lettuce and a quarter segment of tomato . That was the side salad . I think the budget for the side salad department might have been a couple of quid . Maybe a lettuce . And half a dozen tomatoes . They were put on the plate for pure decoration . Never to be consumed . As they collected the plates they would recycle the segment of tomato and leaf of lettuce to the advancing new customers and keep that routine going all day . As kids we would joke that there was 4 different types of condiments on the side salad before it ever reached the table . The Coffee House was ideally located just 20m from Andytown lesiure centre . So you can replenish the body with a nice greasy fry after a workout or a swim . Yummy . Eventually it got turned into a carpet shop and then some wildly ambitious non businessman turned it into an American style Hard Rock Café with a duke box . Big burgers and expensive milkshakes with big prices . The road was changing but not to those extremes and it was unsuccessful . I don't know what sits there now .

The Road that's seen its fair share of violence and riots . The Road an ever flowing hive of activity . Everybody looks in for the next big event . Waiting in defensive mode . For something to happen . I believed that it was me . The next big thing is me . When you're on the Road . You're on display .

Now I was back in my grandfathers . Every night I would go into the front bedroom upstairs and continue with my training regime . I would leave the curtains open . The light from the lamp post across the street would create a shadow in the room against the wall . The room was dark and I would shadow box observing the speed , variety and quickness of punches of my shadow . I would always try and out speed my shadow . In my mind I always made it that I did . My training session would end with 200 sit-ups every night maximum intensity 2-50's 2-30's and 2-20's . I used to limp out of the room every night . It's the only way I could sleep at night . I would find my grandfather in some terrible states . My cousin Tony who lived in the house before me would sometimes carry him up to bed . But I didn't want to touch him . I was afraid of hurting him . Again . His skin draped over that skeleton frame and high cheek bones and me hurting him couldn't of been further from the truth . He was tough as old nails . One night when he was a bit pissed up he had a fall at the front door . The Taxi driver dropped him off from the local club . He was a committee member . He woke up with a shiner and a bit of bruising . For 9 month's he worked and carried on bricklaying with discomfort to his arm . When one of my Aunties took him to the hospital after all that time it turned out there was a serious break in his arm . He was 68 years old . He was a medical marvel . When I was in Afghanistan I got the news that he had passed away . At the end he was suffering from senile dementia . Cheers Granda . You gave me a home when no one else would . And I Thank you .

I acquired a dog within a week of moving in . It just worked out that way . A guy from the neighbourhood was giving her away . I used her as a running partner at night . She was a mix of American Pitbull and a Bullstaff . She was a beast , and a nasty fight with one of her syblings had left her with half an ear and the other one ripped . Infection set in , and wherever Saoirse went a bad smell followed . The smell was rancid . Saorise means freedom in Irish . She was thirteen months old and the previous owner had already squeezed two litters out of her with little recovery time . She had tits like a cow that never stopped producing milk . I'd take her out at night when the roads were empty . She'd stay beside me off the lead and we'd go to Musgrave Park and run around it a couple of times . She loved bursting balls and stripping trees of their branches . We'd run past the old grey Army fortress in Musgrave Park . It was dormant , and on one or two occasions I'd see Police are Army Landrovers leaving them . The Police Landrovers were the same colour as the grey tinned fortress that loomed ugly in Musgrave .

Eventually the PSNI would paint their Landrovers to a peaceful and unthreatening white . They were widely known by some in the community as ice cream vans . I did spend a little bit of time in one of them . A bar at the bottom of my street was burnt down . It was accidentally burnt down . It was called the White Fort . As you can imagine a burnt-down bar became a bit of a gold mine after the flames had been quenched . There was a bit of talk in the street of a few of its regulars who knew the lay out of the pub . They entered and knew where to look and helped themselves . I decided I'd go in the next day in broad day light and have a snoop around , and when I did the Police surrounded the place and I tried to hide . The roof had fell in and there was black soot over everything . The pub smelt horrible . Burnt wood and alcopops . As the Police closed in I stayed low beside a window . I thought I was safe until a huge arm with a black leather glove on it reached in and picked me right up . Right over the window sill and into Police custody . When I hit the station they threw me in a cell . My father let me stay there till late into the night . A lesson . The cell was lonely and joyless and it was filled with frustration . The layout of the cell let you sit nowhere but facing the door ; you couldn't see out but anyone could look in whenever they liked . I didn't enjoy my time in a cell by myself . When I was interviewed I told the Police Officer that I wanted to be a fireman when I was older and simply wanted to check out what a burnt-down building looked like . They warned me and eventually the charges were dropped . I don't think they believed the fireman story . I think the PSNI took pity on me . It was my first and last ever offence .

I would later put down Saorise . Her ears were getting much worse and my aunts and uncles were giving me a hard time about the rancid smell in my grandfather's house . She died in my arms as she shuttered her last breaths . It was only then that I realsied how massive her head actually was . Disproportionately big to her body . She was a beast . My beast . She knew she was being put down . I felt she had had a hard life and she wasn't recovering well . There was only so much progress she could make over the 6 months of owning her . I had a little blue Pug 106 . Fully legit . I would work a Sunday in a Chinese on the Blacks Road delivering food . The reason I worked this Chinese more than anything is that I had a unique relationship with the owners , Ken and Nuala , who were two of the loveliest and hardest-working people you could ever meet . It was a pleasure just to help them out . They were like parental figures to me and I was treated like I was one of their sons . I would of done anything for them and we shared a relationship of genuine trust that was felt and earnt . Using the Pug106 , I loaded Saorise into the car in a heavy black industrial bag , and with a spade I dug a grave and buried her twelve miles outside Belfast in the country . It was the right thing to do . I felt if I couldn't give her a decent life at nineteen months old . A healthy life . 2 gammy ears . Tits like a cow . Was best to put this thing to sleep . She was a loyal companion and had kept me company so many dark , lonely nights while I ran . The dog showed me complete loyalty , as every dog does , and it was the least I could do to honour her existence .

I'd been back in my grandfathers for 6 months and now I started a new routine . I took to running at night about the mountains that surrounded Belfast . The Black mountain . At early o'clock in the morning . I would run up the Mona bypass onto the road that eats into the side of the Black mountain . I would look down on Belfast . It did look beautiful at night . But dead . It lacked an energy that I craved . It wasn't New York . Or London . It was amazingly peaceful and the air was sharp and cold . The country lanes were frightening and never did I bump into another person on them roads . Most of the time I was genuinely frightened . It was dark , scary and shadowy . The imagination plays tricks on the mind . I was alone . Me . Myself . And my fears . Times I would stop breathless and say , ' what the fuck are you doing ' , referring to me being alone on a mountain in pitch black , miles from my home . Making my way back to my grandfathers for 5 O clock in the morning . It would still be dark . I would hear the birds waking up and the M1 which was just 100m away was still quiet because the early morning traffic hadn't woken up yet . The air was crisp and I would feel re-born . Exhausted but reborn . Go straight to bed , not even drinking any water . I would wake up late morning /early afternoon . The days of working for my uncles were coming to an end . I did a little agency work . Warehouse . Or on the road delivering lemonade and alcohol to pubs and supermarkets . I hated Belfast for the lack of opportunities it presented for me . Through connections I found myself gutting out houses that belonged to a wealthy entrepreneur . I worked hard and went the extra mile countless times and he appreciated me and my work ethic . We became close . Even good friends . I adored him for the job he was doing with his 2 kids and stepson , for the respect and loyalty he showed to his wife , Lorean . He set the blueprint of how I would be if I settled down , if any woman would ever have me .

I continued my routine every night . With my return to Andytown came a confidence . It was unmistakable , and that resolve I had earned and proven to myself was immoveable , it existed within me . It was radiated from the depths of my very existence . I was separate from Andytown . No longer felt connected . Obliged . Oppressed . I was my own entity observing everything going on around me . I became self-aware . And what if , just what if I could influence the direction of my life with this new everlasting discovery of what I was capable of physically and mentally . There was two options that burned inside my mind . One was to be a professional boxer , and the other was to join the army and get a career . Coming from Andytown , a hugely Roman Catholic , war torn part of Northern Ireland , I knew that the British Army would not go down too well , so I pursued the Irish Army . As the years went past I realized it was near impossible to join the Irish Army as the waiting list was over a year . And what did the Irish Army ever do anyway . They were shite and never went anywhere . No . If I joined the army I wanted some stories . Not go to Lebanon on a peace keeping tour every couple of years and do nothing .

It's not just the catholic and protestant thing that is an issue . The biggest issue I felt coming from West Belfast was that there was little pockets of gangs . Some of these gangs were up to twenty strong and the gangs used these fierce numbers and reputations to intimidate , bully and give a beating to whoever they liked , or , rather , disliked . Within the gang there was undoubtedly a rank structure also . I was fine in and around my own backyard , but you might walk a mile up or down the Road and encounter a gang that knows nothing about you . Then it's your job to teach them a little bit about yourself , or a lot , depending on what your confronted with . You could find myself walking past a crowd like that on a street corner on a Friday or Saturday night . They've all been drinking and it can turn dangerous . Being outnumbered by huge numbers quicker than you can click your fingers . As quick as a look .

Because of the person I was . I didn't have to walk far to meet resistance like this . It's almost like I had to prove I was this guy to everyone and fight anyone who posed a challenge . I knew that very few people had put themselves through the paces I had . I was prepared to die to get the respect I felt I deserved . This was best personified when I encountered a group of doormen on the Road . They would snarl and stare at me like I was an inconvenience to them . That's a bit cheeky . These particular gentlemen are getting paid £10 an hour standing on my Road throwing daggers and I'm the one that's inconveniencing them . They definitely carried the , *I'm bigger , stronger and scarier than you and I will crush you mentality* . That's wonderful and that might work on 99.99% of the rest of the guys you encounter but guess what I'm that 0.01% that won't tolerate your bullshit . The mentality that goes with that career choice , you can understand how some of the blokes get carried away . Anybody can Knock some poor bastard out who's had eight pints down his neck . Stumbling out the door on his way home . My little feud lasted about two years between four of them . On and off . It escalated to one St Patrick's Day when the whole road was on the Andytown Road drinking . Give an Irishman an excuse for a drink .

I left Riverdale that day knowing that within 5 minutes I would be on the road and I would be fighting this specific doorman . His name was Stevie . He was about twice the size in breadth and width of me and in good shape . On reflection it would be fair to say that he was a master intimidator . He got me fired up . His trick of staring and posturing might of worked on many before but with me I gave him , *The shit stops here vibe* . I could see his frustration at his little trick not working , and I grew confident that me not giving ground would result in a mega clash between he and I that could be fatal for either one of us .

As I walked out of the street I could feel my ears tingling and my head itchy on the top of my scalp . There was people all over the Road and especially drinking in and around were Stevie did the door . As I walked near his location on the other side of the road he started taking his jacket and tie off . As he locked his eyes on me I could feel his glare , glaring through me , glaring right into my soul . I continued ; I was primed for battle and ready to take and give punishment . Butterflies only heightened my awareness . I was ready to die . **'YOU!!!' 'HERE!!!' 'NOW!!!'** . Yeah right mate . You walk to me if you wana battle . Whatever! . A flick of my chin in the direction I choose to go if nobody intercepted me . Still primed for battle .

He's coming……

When he came within 1m of me I steadied myself for the onslaught to come . He moved menacingly . He's a big man . As he came within striking distance a looping right hand was the first thing from his onslaught , I countered that with a straight head butt, straight down the middle it connected and bounced of his chin . The war had commenced it was down to heart , courage , speed , skill and tactics . He threw powerful plodding shots that didn't bludgeon me but moved me 10-15m backwards as I covered up and parried with the shots . The Road was watching and before I knew it I had a cut opened over my right eye . The blood was warm and troubled my vision . A little breather from his end , I quickly took off my sweater , dabbed my eye – Gleaming , the cut was trickling now .

As he approached me for another onslaught , I breathed in and seized the moment . He wasn't even feinting anymore , and he came for me with his hands closer to his chest than his chin . I dug my feet in and threw a perfect crisp punch , right hand , straight down the pipeline as it crunched a couple of inches in and through his chin . I could feel every muscle in my body work towards landing and executing that shot , and it was delivered so crisply corked and retracted in a nanosecond , that his eyes done a funny stir and he took 2 or 3 steps back . The fight was over . I never got any trouble of them doormen again after that , and I spent most of that night in Queen Victoria Hospital getting fixed up .

In some street fights I've been unwittingly called over to a crowd in very amicable terms . Even though I know that the crowd may not particularly like me , the terms are amicable . A crowd of up to 8 , and then when I approach the main man who wants to have a beef with me , the leader of the crowd he's landed 3 or 4 sneaky little sharp , snappy hooks on my jaw before I even realize what's going on . The crowd of 8 quickly become a circle of 7 , with myself and the main man in the middle . On this occasion I sense my opponent has a kickboxing background , and as I come in he's locked both my arms under his . He's taller than me and I lower the top of my head tight under his chin . If I can't start letting shots go in the inside I want my head and chin tucked in on his chest , to protect it . Then I start feeling a strange sensation on the back of my head while my head and chin are tucked below his . He's biting me on the back of my head . A little voice inside my head says *, Now this fuckers biting me ?* . I step back as I forcefully release my arms , and push him away from me at the same time .

I can see he's looking for me to engage , but he's taller than me with longer reach , and probably physically slightly stronger . I want him to fight my fight . He started this and he's in front of all his friends , so the pressures on him to look good and finish what he's started , and if he can't finish it he's gona look like a prat in front of his mates . I want to counter . I want him to charge in but he's surprisingly patient . If he opens up he leaves me openings of which I can hit hard single hurtful shots , or stinging combos . Depends how loose his guard is . As he advances , that's when he's vulnerable . I'll pick him off with something hurtful , and stingy . My boney corking shots . He edges slightly closer to get his range . Again , patiently , I edge slightly out of it . I don't want him to effortlessly slip into punching range . Or kicking range . I know now by his movement he does have a kickboxing background , as his stance is square on . This pricks started it . You got 3 lucky shots . Now put me in my place . You sneaky Bitch . Now it's on . Test my chin . It'll have to be a surge from you . Come forward . I want you to . Come quickly , I want you to feel my boney , stingy , corking shots . As I edge back once too many times I trip over a bike that's been dropped by some kid , who's keen to look in . This is his chance to assert his dominance . He does a big leaping , fly – kicking , stamp attempt . I get from my back to my feet , in 3 swift movements , and I keep distance by maneuvering away from him , instead of forward . It takes less than ½ a second . A move I learnt in a MMA keep fit class . Then I fall right into my stance with my hands high . And then as quickly as it's started , it's over . He walks away with his crowd . And I'm left feeling , rather disappointed , even saddened . My resilience has been tested and there's no point continuing but what he has started is suddenly unresolved . No one has been beaten into submission or hurt . When that happens you're left with that much emotion , that has nowhere to be channeled , especially because the confrontation was rather unexpected to begin with . There is no victor , and your emotional well is that full and on the brink that a sudden and unresolved ending can be very overwhelming . It's very possible to cry , just to release some of what's built up inside you . Behind closed doors and away from the Road of course . When you cut around Andytown the way I do . People will observe you . Get themselves fired up and ready and then have a go . People will challenge you . To me Andytown was a Battlefield . A psychological Battlefield .

I was always fighting bigger guys on the Road . Guys who outweighed me , out-reached me and who were physically stronger . Always guys with reputations of being handy , who come to fight and prove a point . With these guys you have to have fighting intelligence and hurt them with sweet shots . If I was fighting someone my own size , weight and frame I could hurt them and let go with combos . Cuffing shots that can put them and keep them off balance and then overwhelm them with cleaner , more effective blows . I was never in a 50/50 fight when it came to size , weight and strength , and I preferred it that way . Otherwise . What's the point .

I kept in touch with the crowd from Twinbrook : Doyler , Tony , Phil . But I was bored of it . All of it . The whole scene . None of them had any vision . They were content to work all week just so they could party at the weekend and repeat the process over and over and over again . I was reading a lot of self-help books . Sometimes 4 books a week . I knew I wouldn't have my youth forever . I needed to do something with my life . I didn't want to end up like my father under an engine and battling cancer at the same time . (Only I would more likely be on a building site , very unhappy and just working to get by) . I wasn't living a life . I was asking God for answers and I knew eventually that if I stayed in Belfast then Belfast would determine my fate and it wouldn't be joyish or fruitful . There was a furnace inside me . Burning . I wanted more than what I was getting . I wanted meaning . I wanted purpose . And as I became more and more detached from the group I got more and more aggro from the group

' You think your better than us or something... '

No . I'm not better than you or anybody else . I'm just a lot better than this and what you people are making me out to be . I'm so much more than what you're making me out to

75

be . A drinking buddy . Someone to score drugs with to rub your ego in a drug-induced slur . My time with the boys revealed that I had a very high tolerance level for the drug ecstasy . They would of all took 10 and be smacked out , pulling faces that would haunt a house . I would take twice that many , sometimes 20 in one night , and be in control , enjoying it , very much keeping it together . Obviously enjoying and feeling the effects of the drug coursing through my blood . I am no way recommending this to anyone . I did it for 2 reasons . I have an extreme personality and I like to push myself and my body to the limit . And secondly , I was very unhappy within the group , and felt used and undervalued , and the drug acted as some sort of relief , some escapism . Many times we ended up in Lady Dixon , climbing trees , or up in the country in Leathemstown reservoir for a nice cool refreshing swim . I knew this reservoir well ; as a kid , me and my mates used to go up to it in summertime with our rods and bait and clean it out of its brown trout . As kids we called these brown trout brownies .

My final decision to end my association with the boys from the Twinbrook days fell with Doyler . We were drinking out his back one day . He suddenly in great detail described a story from his childhood . He'd been playing football in the street and the ball had repeatedly gone into his neighbours' garden . This is when he was a kid . The neighbour came out . Took his ball and told him to' *Fuck Off away from the front of the house'* . That was fair enough , but then Doyler described the story like this

' *So I pretended to strangle myself* ' . In front of me and everyone he wrapped his perfectly manicured hands around his neck and demonstrated how he strangled himself .

' *So there would be marks on my neck like he'd done it* ' . He was referring to the neighbour .

' *I went and told my Ma and she went down and started punching him* ' . He demonstrated his mother throwing punches , flailing away with his delicate-looking banker's hands and thin wrists , and then gave a sneaky and disturbing little laugh .

When I heard this my heart sank and I found it hard to hide my disgust . I couldn't believe what I was hearing . After all this time , how could he reveal something like this . I couldn't believe what was coming out of his mouth . We're talking about a twenty-six- year old man . I've trusted this person enough to invite him into my personal life . He finished the story with ,

' *I'm Spiteful You Know* '

When I heard this I thought *Who the fuck is this* . I wasn't raised like that . The story went against everything I was raised **not to be** . To be spiteful . Make your mummy fight your battles . I knew then that I had to get away from this crowd , especially because Doyler was one of the main players because of his age , the money and the control he had over other members of the group because of the way he done business with them . It must have been important for him to be seen that way . Big fish . Small pond . A group in which I had ended up simply by virtue of getting thrown out of my grandfather's house when I was seventeen and having nowhere else to live . Simply because they were using the flat in Twinbrook as a party flat . I decided after that that Doyler had a very toxic personality . Though after that little intervention I still considered him a friend , even though I knew our friendship was on an egg-timer . I couldn't have someone with this lack of values close to me in the long run . Back then I was too nice , too eager to please . If I did have a weakness it was not ending toxic or damaging relationships in good time . When he first took the effort to put his arm around me and declare we were best mates I took it literally and not for what it was . A con . The only things keeping me in Belfast was the dog and my friendship with Doyler . I'd killed off the dog . I had a soft spot for Doyler since Twinbrook . I'd kept contact with mostly him since moving back to Andytown . Out of the whole group he was the only one I felt I could trust . Be completely open and honest with . He could trust me also . I'd sensed that these negative traits were there in Doyler all along . Below the surface . But never had he been so forward about it . So open about this affliction to his character . I sensed he was almost resetting expectations of what to expect from him . Honestly , he was already a bit of an arsehole at times . But manageable .

I was engaged and invested in my friendship with Doyler . We had a friendship that I valued and it was hard to walk away from . It really was . We were very familiar with each other's company . Four years . He was a wheeler-dealer and aloof , someone who liked to drift around from party to party . He'd heard of someone in the neighbourhood who disliked me immensely . He bumped into him at a house party . Of course they got talking . Of course I already knew about this person . You just know who has a genuine dislike for you . It's a small community and you can pick them feelings up through the stratosphere . Lying in bed or while you make a cup of tea . You can pick it up from a look . Or someone's physiology when they sense your presence , but Doyler took it a step further to try and feed my imagination . Have some fun with it . When he described what *HE* imagined this person would want to do to me *HE* described it like this : ' *He hates you that much he'd want to stab you* ' .

He was cleaning his Lexus outside his mothers' at the time . He was close to me . Made a hand movement towards my abdominal area , a stabbing motion . As if he was doing it himself , all the time sneering , looking right into my eyes . Like he was enjoying it . He turned away quickly to resume cleaning his car , leaving me with the thought . As he was cleaning his Lexus outside his mothers' house I thought it best to walk away and not make a scene . At first I was disgusted with myself that I could put myself in a position where anyone could talk to me like that . Then I thought , Fuck it . This little cunts taking liberties . I texted him

' You really piss me off , talking to me like that '

Doyler ,' *What do you mean* '

' Stabbed '

' That's what I mean '

' You've got some balls talking to me like that '

Doyler , ' *Oh Fuck Off* . *Everyone knows you're just jealous of me* '

' Jealous ? Name one quality you have that I'd be jealous of you , Fucking Phony '

He stupidly replied something about doing a burnout in his Lexus . Jealous!!What?? . He didn't challenge me . He challenged my pocket . My father used to tell me that clothes didn't make the man , and through the process of our friendship Doyler **must** of come to dislike me . Simple as that . But I instantly took it to a sub-conscious level that he'd like to see me killed or just stabbed . Thoughts are things . So are other people's . Never let anyone psychologically push you around . Manage you verbally like this : ' *Stabbed* ' or ' *Jealous* ' . Mention such things likes it's par for the course . My best advice to anyone who's ever confronted with this : Fight this stuff like your life depends on it . Never let anyone box you in with nonsense like this because if you do you won't have a life . Doyler couldn't beat snow of a rope so the only thing he could do is fuck with my head . Ok . You wana fuck with my head . Let's go with this . He was my friend for nearly half a decade . Four years . I considered it a betrayal of the trust I had instilled in the friendship . These are the kinds of characters I had in my life from my time in Twinbrook . It did impact me harder because around that time I was asking myself very real questions about my future in Belfast and was very open to whatever was out there . That's what happens when you hit the precipice from living somewhere all your life and your plan to get out hasn't manifested itself yet . You leave yourself open for anything to come your way and you ask God , you mix that with a steady assertiveness and things happen . Doyler maybe sensed this and tried to fill my void with his bullshit . If I ever felt someone was going for something that would better themselves or their life , they would be met with encouragement and a warm word . I still always secretly really wanted to go to Dutch Harbour . *The Deadliest Catch* . And catch king crabs on those rough and treacherous seas . Sixteen-hour days . Eight weeks' work . Come back with tens of thousands of pounds . But I was a long way away from Alaska and I didn't have the reddies to get started .

If Doyler had pulled that stunt much earlier in the friendship I'd of laughed and told him to split , but after four years it was very snidey . The comment was so unusual . At first I was dumbfounded and didn't know what way to react . I was angry but felt he was pitiful also . The initial insult is that someone you've befriended is directly telling you that they are better than you . But why would one be jealous of a lesser man . According to Doyler *' Everyone knew it '* . To put it mildly , I thought it dangerous for him to be talking about such stuff so casually . I didn't like the connotations for my character . The connotations being that I would lower to such a degree and that a brat of Doyler's stature would be my affixation . You'd need to be pretty special for me to be jealous of you . The accusation nearly blew my mind . Where did he get that idea from . Maybe because he had a Lexus and I didn't . Maybe he thought I was getting too big for my boots . Maybe I was getting a bit too much attention for his liking . Because of the noise I was making on the Road . And maybe he

couldn't compete with what was going on inside me .
Maybe . His attack was delivered so surgically with such
venom that it wasn't a stretch to imagine that it was pre
planned .

I didn't have time to be jealous . Didn't have time to adopt
that emotion . Most of my time in Andytown before I went
to Twinbrook , I felt like I was drowning . These invisible
forces that exist . Trying to drag me down . The visceral
energy that smoothers that road . I was very sensitive to
that energy on the Road as an adolescent .This drowning
feeling comes from being round small-minded people like
Doyler , who are trying to wrap you in *their* shit . People
who don't have your best interests at heart . You can either
give up and be swept away with it and along with it or you
can swim and escape ; but when you're drowning there's
no room for jealousy . Just survival . So jealousy was never
ever there . Never in my make-up . There was people that I
admired , but Doyler wasn't one of them . Certainly not
after this little revelation .

The people I admired . The people I replicated . Elite
prizefighters with punching power and auras of invincibility
. Not just from my era . The Ray Robinsons . The Jersey Joe
Walcotts and The Jack Dempseys . Archie Moore . I loved
Archie Moore , the Old Mongoose . The greatest light
heavyweight ever . He moved up to heavyweight and
dropped the Great Marciano before eventually getting
knocked out . These guys I admired . Not some brat who
strangles himself so his mummy can fight his battles . When
I was in my grandfather's front bedroom in pitch black ,
shadowboxing observing my shadow on the wall , I'd be

thinking of all the great fighters from the past . Having the cunning , guile and ring generalship of Jersey Joe Walcott . Having the intensity and punching power of Nigel Benn . The ferocity of Jack Dempsey . The heart of Archie Moore . The fluidity of Marco Antonio Barrera throwing shots . I would fill myself with these thoughts . I carried these fighters in my heart everywhere I went . The courage and human quality that all these fighters showed inspired me .

I didn't mind Doyler talking a lot of stuff behind my back . That's just the type of character he was . I knew he did , and it didn't bother me , it really didn't . But don't ever look me square in the eye and talk about me being stabbed with glee . He was gaining strength talking to me like this . Him even suggesting , much less trying to convince me that ' everyone knew I was jealous of him ' was a serious challenge to my masculinity . Of course he knew he was wet , soft and pampered and that I wasn't . It was time to reset the boundaries . Put this child in his box .I meditated on him for 3 days . I thought of all the nasty negative things he had said to me . It took me 3 days to undo a 4 year friendship . For them 3 days I was in the moment ready to be confronted by him or confront him . He kept his distance and when he did approach he did sheepishly with a small demeanor .' *We may as well be friends again* ' . I shook his hand and looked at him ' You had your chance ' . And he's lucky he did approach me like this because my intentions for him were not that of peace and love . A lot of people reading this might think , Why didn't you just ignore him? I'm from a small , close knit community were everybody knows everyone's business . To ignore a jibe like this would open the floodgates for much more . From much lesser men . It was typical that at the eleventh hour , when there was no other option , but to fight and back up all his talk , he flaked . I'm surprised he didn't get his mummy for me .

When it comes to people , I don't do half relationships . I'm an all or nothing type of guy and I see things through right till the end . If someone has exposed themselves to be fraudulent and untrustworthy , I discard them from my life . I don't start anything I won't finish .They were all stagnant and happy . I wanted more . Much more . I was better off alone . From that day on I took a more assertively aggressive stance in my life and **absolutely** controlled who I let into my life . I wanted out . Life is not worth living if I don't leave this place , I thought . It's just not worth living , if I don't leave this place .

Evolving – testing the boundaries

Andytown's a place where if you get too big there'll be a que of 100 that'll come out of the woodwork to cut you down to size to restore the balance , verbally , psychologically and physically . Belfast in the whole is a notoriously tough place . Working class Belfast will either break or enforce one's resolve . The majority just get on with it . Like my father . They don't know any other way . It's hard for everyone , and if someone is perceived to have more physically or financially or any other way it can create jealousy and envy . These are natural human emotions but when the terrain is much tougher than the norm these emotions are amplified much more , much higher and much quicker .

I got it in my head that if I were to walk down the centre of Andytown road with my six-pack bulging , my arms cocked , with a clear mind and pure heart , then , if this were to take place and nobody approached me then psychologically I would have conquered Andytown and the demons keeping me there . As I did it , I could feel God's presence . It was extremely intense and I felt him smiling as I strutted my stuff . I believe God favours the brave . The ones who stand up and be counted . The ones who look deep inside and in return . **THEY** inspire others .

I walked down the center of Andytown Road . The length of it . Poised for battle . My top off . I wanted to be confronted . Ridiculed . Challenged . Laughed at . Hurt physically . I walked slowly and purposefully , soaking in every look , every stare , every look of amazement . I was ripped , strong , fit and aggressive , with a will to succeed . I was in great shape . It was reminiscent of Chris Eubank . When he does his Ring walk . I was a big Eubank fan . The way he spat out defiance , I could relate . I was ready for my creator , anybody , to strike me down . I was rebelling , breaking the rules , non conformist . Nothing happened . I'm a God . This is my universe . This is my town . It's my time . I was Bruce Lee . Better still , I was Colum Francis McGeown the first . I was untouchable . I was in a universe of my own . Nobody was close . I was twenty-two years old . Where was my degree , my opportunities , my Frank Warren , my escape plan from this life of bleak oppression . Cold , wet , grey , opportunity-less Belfast . I wasn't to succumb to working-class Belfast . Not now . Not ever . Not without a fight till the death . I raged a war with the demons within me , with the injustices suffered by my people , not political , poverty , alcoholism , joblessness , on benefits , on the dole , black taxi's driving in and out of the city better known as the Town for a pound a head , living in council housing .

A Place that tells you where you can or can't go if you are a certain religion is oppression . Boundaries . Walls . Why were people living like this ? Where was the sunshine ? Where was the Hope ?

I became the hope I wanted to see . My strength and resolve was unmatched . I looked around me , I had no time for the people who had settled , mitigated , accepted . I looked inside . I was enraged . I was ready . Nobody was going to get in my way ; if they did I was going to kill or maim them . I'm getting the fuck out of here and nobody will stop me . I have nothing left to fear ; staying here is death .

You try walking down the centre of Andytown Road like this with a glimmer of doubt , and somebody would stop their car and hit you a slap on the way to work . When no one approached me or laughed , I knew I'd conquered my Town and most importantly my demons .

FINDING SALVATION

Family politics and my mother and father splitting up
meant the family home was sold , money was split and my
mother moved into my grandfather's to live and look after
her father . Two days later I was in the Salvation Army in
the center of Belfast . I was twenty-two and a half years old
. I didn't want to be around my mother . She'd of did my
head in . When I first weighed into the Salvation Army I was
amazed at the energy in the place . It seemed like a place
where people were actually helped and willing to help a
soul in need . I thought you'd of been treated like an
outcast because you were homeless and had no were to go
. It was the opposite : you were treated with kindness and
concern . I had a little interview with a girl called Rosemary
. Rosemary had a good soul . A lovely woman in her early to
mid forties and I was very pleased when she decided to
give me a room . Our first meeting she mentioned housing
for me and my ears did prick up . She continued ,' I could
get you a house in Tigers Bay tomorrow but you wouldn't
last a night ' . Me being me I said ' I'll live in Tigers Bay ' .
She smiled and took a look at me . Tigers Bay is a fiercely
Protestant community . When referring to rough places ,
my mother always used to say , ' Such and such a place –
They eat their young ' . Tigers Bay is one of these areas ,
especially if you're an outsider coming from say Andytown
of Falls Road . There are plenty of places in the West where
' They eat their young ' also . Twinbrook and Ballymurphy

could hold such stigma , no doubt . This might be hard for someone not from Northern Ireland to understand , but I can identify someone from the other side of the fence quicker than a second and they can do the same with me . You know your own and you know who isn't . Just like someone from Sandy Row , The Shankill or Tigers Bay would take one look at me and know I was a rough , tough kid from either The Falls Road or Andytown direction .

More than that they would of seen me for what I am , ' A Fenian ' . I'm happy with that , I'd call myself a Celtic warrior any day of the week . In the crudest possible way they could be known as a ' Hun ' or a ' Prod ' . But this is the crudest of ways of which I never was , and I would never associate or label anyone this . To people who grow up here , it's as easy as spotting someone who's black or from an oriental origin . Little tell-tale signs I could use to identify someone from the other side . If a kid has a middle shade or bleached blonde hair on top . Me moving into Tigers Bay , Rosemary was right : it would not of been a lengthy or fruitful endeavour . The suggestion was taken away as quickly as it was introduced . Just having a room to myself was the most I could've ever hoped for .

The room had light blue lilo squared tiles , high ceiling , a wooden built-in wardrobe , a single plastic coathanger attached to the inside of the door , and a little wooden unit that you could place a TV on if you had one . The little unit was perfect size if you were to sit on bed and watch TV . The TV would be at eye level . The room had enough space to walk around in and not feel cramped .

I had everything inside me to succeed . And now I had a base to operate from . I loved the town at night . I had never witnessed the town from that perspective , completely empty and desolate of people . I loved running through it . I shopped in Primark . Picking up cheap trainers for a fiver . They were the best running shoes I ever had .Expensive shoes like Nike and Adidas are built for comfort . My feet were tough as nails and I enjoyed running , pounding the road and feeling more connected . I would let my hair and beard grow and focus solely on my body and my mind . I loved waking up in my own room and feeling the lactic acid in my legs . I was addicted to that feeling , so pushed myself harder and harder for longer and longer when running so I could still feel the effects of that recovery process . The Lagan tow path was the common route I ran during the day .

In the evening I patrolled the reception area and TV area , refusing to befriend anyone . If anyone wanted to be my friend they would come to me . I was self-contained , and a friendship with me could only benefit the other person , in my mind . It wasn't but a week in that I met Victor . Victor was a round shape with a round bull head . He was built like a bull , a big boy , with grey receding hairline shaved tight to his round bull head , and being a county Fermanagh man he carried a broad southern Irish accent . He was mid forties and had a bit of knowing and a little bit of menace about him . I was drawn to him . And he to I . We shook hands and sat down for a game of chess . He check mated me in three moves . 'Bastard!' I said . How did he do that . Victor explained that he'd just recently been released from jail after a ten-year stretch for armed robbery and he couldn't return to where he lived before because his landlord had thrown the rope up and the block of flats he lived in before he had been incarcerated had been torn down . I took him at his word . It Seemed plausible .

My morning ritual was 3 and 1/2 - 7 miles . I would warm up across from the Salvation Army , outside the Northern Bank . Greeting people who walked past me . I noticed that a lot of the guys from the games room would observe me ; Victor was one of them . And when I rocked in that night , from that night on Victor and I became good friends . There was another who would drift in and out of Victor and myself's company . His name was Ali and he was a Muslim . Victor used to call him Ali Baba . He was a tall , dark , handsome Indian guy who did not get on with his father . He was rebelling against his father and his father's businesses . As the eldest son he was making his statement , and at one stage for a short time the three of us were inseparable . We had interesting methods how to find money . We would claim compensation from the brew , crisis loans , and rock up to St Vincent de Paul in tatty clothes with both arms the one length with a story about being hungry and getting a little £10 or £20 voucher for the Tesco up the street , and when we had money we would shop in shops were the pound goes further . The towns littered with little shops like that .

After a couple of weeks I was boxing in three different gymnasiums in Belfast each week and running some weeks up to a hundred miles . Up to eighteen or twenty miles a day . I did this at a strong , intense , fast pace . I was an animal . In the boxing gyms I would spar with anybody Big , little or large . I would practice on things in the ring , and if I was in with somebody smaller I would just feint with my right hand and touch him with my jab just enough to get him to respect me , but usually I let the smaller , younger guys beat up on me . It felt good , and with the smaller , quicker guys I would perfect my speed of movement . Some of the Gyms were in West Belfast and I would run back into town nearly seven miles . I was drawn to the speed ball and could control it for up to two or three minutes at a fanatic pace ; but what brought me most pleasure apart from sparing was bullying the heavy bag around with jabs and quick combos to head and body , all with fluidity . I loved the feeling off my hands smashing something with super-quick power and speed continuously and having it in me to keep that intensity going all day .

It's an amazing feeling , knowing that you can really hurt someone with your hands , guys twice your size . Walking around with that feeling all the time , you almost feel guilty for what you can do , with your hands .

Each room in the Hostel was like a little cell . I had a window view overlooking the only Gay Bar in Belfast . On particular nights it would be drag night and some nights I would hear some of the gays making a lot of noise , screaming and shouting . Fighting with each other . I'm one for watching a fight between two supreme physical athletes with insurmountable physical courage and confidence in their ability . A couple of little gays arguing after seeing their partner flirting or kissing another gay boy – unfortunately that ain't it . That's not what constitutes a fight in my world . I would close my window to drown out the noise and go get a cup of tea and some Minstrels out of the tea and chocolate vending machine . They were all reasonably priced . Twenty p . for a cup of Kenco , PG tea or Hot Chocolate , all in little cups . Forty p. for Minstrels , Twix or a packet of Barbecue Hunky Dorys . Tea and Minstrels was my guilty pleasure . I had a sweet tooth because of the physical training I was doing . I would sometimes devour whole jars of Nutella at a time . My body literally craved this sweet stuff ; ready-made custard from Tesco was one of my favorites too .

In the canteen the meals were a Pound at breakfast , lunch and dinner . Breakfast usually consisted of one bacon , one sausage , one fried egg with bread and butter . I think beans may have been on the menu . I ate in the canteen the first two weeks . I loved it . I thought it was great value . After two weeks the limitation became clear . The food was either Heavily boiled , i.e. The goodness was boiled out of it , or fried so it was dripping with grease . I was training that hard that my body was craving foods that it really needed . Red meats , white meats , which I cooked on a George Foreman . I bought it with the £10 or £20 Argos gift voucher the Hostel gave everyone for Christmas , and made up the difference out of my brew money . One day I got a crisis loan from the brew and bought a pair of 12oz boxing gloves I had my eye on for a month . They were in the window of the Martial Arts shop in Town . They were crocodile skin colour and cost me £37 . I loved breaking them in . There was a new build happening round the corner from the Hostel . At this stage it was at the foundations , but when finished the building would lay claim to being the tallest building in Belfast City . *WOW!!*

*Give yourself a pat on the back . Tallest building in Belfast ,
what a fucking achievement!!* . The ply was three metres
high around the whole build . It was perfect for shoe-
shining , practicing my double-jab right hand , single-jab
and right hand . Within two weeks the gloves were bust .

From the hours of nine to twelve in the morning you had to
be out of your room . They claimed it was to clean , but a
brush and mop never hit my floor unless I used it myself .
The Real reason : they would check for drugs and alcohol ,
for which you could be kicked out . The hostel was dry .
Because of this there was an ever flowing stream of people
coming , going . This little rule , nine to twelve , was a little
bit of routine also .

Victor would tell me of someone he knew who started in a
burger van and now owned three old people's homes and
all sorts of businesses that all originated from the burger
van . We would walk and talk for hours . Along my running
route . The Lagan Tow Path . There was even a promise that
one day if I was ever settled and had my own place I would
get the hawker's licence for the burger van and all the food
and hygiene certificates , move Victor over and do it for
real . When we weren't walking and talking , we'd go into
Town to a little coffee kiosk in the middle of Castle Street .
Just opposite McDonald's and Primark . They did the best
coffees and we'd each get a cappuccino , mine with a shot
of cinnamon , Victor liked almond . They were so rich and
tasty and cost the tail end of £3 , and on cold mornings
when we were out of our rooms between nine and twelve
we always greeted the guy who served us with big smiles
and assertive banter .

' What's your Game , Are yous millionaires? '

I guess we were . Millionaires without a penny in our pockets . We kept it going for a while . Victor enjoyed keeping it going the most . ' We'll just keep that fucker guessin' , ' he used to say .

I did have a couple of quid . I had an Ulster Bank credit card that I would tap into , and if Victor ever needed tobacco there was a café we knew off in the Town where we'd meet a guy who did a run from Calais to Dover . He'd bring back huge quantities of Golden Virginia , packs of twenty-five grammes for a fiver , bargain . He would sit in the café at certain times , dish it out , make his money , and then go home and repeat the routine . It was my treat to Victor . What's the price of a packet of Golden Virginia between friends .

After many long-distance walks with Victor , him being nearly twice my age and a good few stone heavier , his legs became a bit busted , so one day he decided to mill around the hostel for them couple of hours until twelve in the afternoon , before being allowed to go to his room . I went for a walk by myself round to the mouth of the River Lagan , near the Odessy Arena side . The mouth of the river is two hundred metres from the hostel . There were a bunch of old fellas jumping on a paddling boat . They used the paddling boat to paddle out to the main fishing boat , which was anchored in the middle of the channel . They'd already pushed off from the side , but I thought I'd chance my arm , ' Is there room for one more? ' As they paddled 2

controlled strokes towards the main boat , they stopped . '
You sure? ' replied an old and heavily white-bearded man . '
Yeah , If you don't mind . '

' We'll be out for a couple of hours . '

' I don't mind . I live in that Hostel round the corner . Got
nothing to do anyway . '

The old bearded man , who went by the name of Vincent ,
rowed back towards the Lagan side and stopped under a
steel ladder fixed into the wall of the river embankment . It
ran a good length down . I climbed down and jumped on ,
aided by a hand from Vincent . We rowed out . I Jumped on
deck and assisted with the untying of the chain from one
boat and tying the paddle boat to the buoyancy ball , and
then we made our way towards open sea . I was given a rod
with three little lures on it . I knew the drill . Mackerel bite
at anything , the tip of a finger , the tin foil from a KitKat
wrapper - but not that day , and after a relaxing and
scorching hot day with them fine older folks we exchanged
numbers and Vincent told me I was welcome anytime .
Again , it wasn't Dutch Harbour . The sun was out and we
weren't going for king crabs , but Vincent was a nice man
and for that day it was a nice break from my physical
routine .

My Aunt Janet lived in South Belfast , about a three and a
half mile jog . I would make my way to hers with
ingredients in my bag and she would let me use her kitchen
to cook . I would make pasta with sauce , bacon and cheese
through it , and make enough for myself and Victor . I

would make a special batch for Ali without the bacon , as he was a devoted Muslim . They loved it . They said it was soul food .

A very unusual thing happened when I was in the Sally Ann : I met a guy called Albert . He was basically a Bible-thumper and he walked with a limp because he lived a life of crime before he found God . He lived in the hostel and was a bit of a character . One could even say a bit of a Jack the lad . He told me that before he found God he use to rob post offices , bookies , businesses . He became that good at it that he attracted the attention of a certain group of people who have a political and financial interest in their respected communities , and when he refused to steal for them they blew both his kneecaps off . So Albert was very convincing in everything he said about his religion , and he followed the book to a tee . He had read the bible cover to cover many times . There was a prayer room and he asked me to join him one day . Sure , no problems , I'm in for new experiences . We went alone and he sat beside me . It was very personal and he simply asked , ' Can I pray for you? ' . I was bemused , if not a little embarrassed and vulnerable . ' Yeah , sure ' , I said . He finished praying and he said , ' Now Colum , I'm gona ask you if you wana accept Jesus into your heart . All you have to say is " Yes " and it'll change your life forever ' . I hesitated but went with it . He'd been kind to pray for me personally and give me his undivided time . I said a full heartedly ' Yes ' , and a warm glow entered me and for about fifteen minutes I felt invincible . I felt the presence of God .

Ali once took me to a mosque . It was very peaceful . A billion people doing them prayers six times a day . There's something in it . He tried to revert me back to Islam . See , Muslims believe that everyone is born a Muslim , so you can't be converted to something you've always been but in their eyes you can be reverted back to Islam .

Albert and Ali were so into their religion Victor would get it going between the Bible and the Koran and let them fight it out . It was good entertainment but the arguments became really heated sometimes , with one of them flaring up and storming off . Victor was good at being the puppetmaster . Ali Baba and Albert the Bible-basher , two good souls . The hostel was great craic and there was characters coming and going every week . It was an ever-changing process and it was great to perform and get the craic going . Don't get me wrong some , nutcases cutting around with some serious issues also . But it felt like I belonged , even though I was in a Hostel that was full of peadophiles and scumbags . A lot of the people were just down on their luck like myself , Victor and Ali , and as I left I would get a smile and a nice word from Stevie , John or Deirdre who worked the front door . Not a feeling of I was under somebody's rules and rules that were unfair and biased towards anyone who wasn't the owner or master of the house , like my father's or Packie's , but *my* house - *My* rules mentality .

Packie even came into my grandfather's house ordering me to put the kettle on , proclaiming that I was merely a lodger in his father's house - in his eyes still under his imaginary control . He wasn't even kind or pleasant about it , he was downright disrespectful and I found myself many times biting my lip . In fact I became used to biting my lip . It would just make me train harder and focus better on how to get out of the situation and Belfast in general . Everything bad in my life I associated with Belfast ; I wanted to escape and never come back . Period . In the Hostel I didn't feel this pressure . I was my own man .

It was here in this predicament that the Army became a very real prospect . I was sick of humping cold wet blocks on the building sites . So I thought , Enough of the hard work , I'll be a dental nurse in the Dental corps of the British Army . You believe that , a dental nurse . It didn't matter , anyway , they paid for my travel out to Aldershot and I flunked the interview . I went into the TV room and lounge when I came back from England and arrived back at the hostel . It was late and I'd been on my feet all day . Everyone in the hostel had retired for the night . I went up to the third floor . Victor was still up . He might have been waiting for me . ' So how'd it go Mcgoo? ' . ' I don' know I'll find out tomorro , ' I replied . I was called out to Palace Barracks . My recruiting officer , Taff , was like ' You fucked the interview , didn't ya ' . I just nodded , I guess I did .

Taff said , ' That's cool , you said you're into running and boxing - maybe dental nurse isn't your thing ... The Irish Guards are recruiting right now . ' He made it sound like a once every ten year event . He went into rhetoric about the regiment . About how I'd be standing at Buckingham Palace and American and Chinese women tourists would be putting their phone numbers in my pockets . I wasn't impressed . He started changing his pitch . ' And you don't even have to do that if you don't want to - once you pass out of training you can go straight to the boxing team and just box for the battalion and be a tracksuit soldier ' . I had already done my little one-day assessment for the dental nurse fiasco . ' So when can I join , Taff? ' ' Here's your joining instructions . ' He handed me a booklet about the regiment and all the timings of where I needed to be and when . I was to start my basic training 25th February 2007 , a week after my twenty-third Birthday .

The people from the Hostel gave me something that resembled a Granny Flat . The whole idea was that this would be your final step on your way out . A little flat with your own sleeping area , kitchen , dining area , shower and bathroom . The rent was something stupid like £5 a week while a hundred metres away there were these luxury apartments worth between £500,000 to a million or more , with exactly the same view . It was in theory so you could hone or establish home keeping skills before you go back out into the real world . They knew my plans about the Army , and liked me , so I think they were trying to make things as comfortable for me as possible before I left . Paradoxically , though , comfort was not on my agenda .

One week before I left , I went to see my father . I felt stronger when I excluded him from my life . He had just moved into a new house since the split with my mother . He was in six months , and none of us had darkened his door , for our own individual reasons . Apart from Victor and the people in the Hostel , he was the first one I told . I went into his house. The house was cold and lifeless . He might have made himself a sandwich . There was bread and cheese out , and there might of been a half-drunk cup of tea . I was sporting a beard and some new clothes from Primark . ' I'm going into the Army , Irish Guards . ' He looked at me , I continued before he could talk .' There's fuck all for me here . I've already signed up and I'm leaving in a week , I'm going . ' I could speak this freely because I knew that no matter what he thought it would have no bearing : in a week I would be on a plane and in my mind I was never coming back . ' Well what about your brothers and sisters ? It's not what happens to you it's what happens to the people you leave behind . ' ' Da , I'm going , there's fuck all for me , I'm fucking homeless . Listen , I just called to tell you that I'm going , that's why I called in . That's all . '

He nodded in acceptance that I was going whether he agreed with it or not . It was a mutual feeling between two men who had hit a crossroad in each of their own lives , going their own ways . I walked off and jumped in a black taxi towards the Town .

Family trouble

A couple of months before , my cousin had moved into the hostel . His name was Gary . He was mixed race . He more or less followed me in . He was a fucking parasite , suck you dry of your energy if you let him get his own way . I wasn't the only one to think he was : Victor disliked him immensely . He used to tell me , ' That little fucker , you watch out for him , he's a hateful little fucker , he's the type that could tell a lie and then prove it . ' I could see were Victor was coming from . He *was* hateful . One day he would wear a Celtic top and the next day he would wear a Rangers top . For the whole time he lived in the Hostel he wore a black Adidas tracksuit ; he never washed it and it was dripping of him . He met Albert , and Albert herded him up with the rest of the sheep to the Tabernacle were some old Paisleyite would be giving a sermon , and within a week he was talking in tongues . ' Talking in shite more like it , ' Victor used to say .

That week leading up to me jumping on the plane to go start my basic , he really stuck it on me . To put it in a nutshell , when I was in the Hostel I was the Guvnor , but instead of waiting till I left to step up , Gary thought he'd give me hell . Conquer . Divide . And destroy . Before leaving , I'd distanced myself from Albert . He'd helped me , but was coming on too strong with the Bible shit . And I had limits . I won't be tamed by no book . So Gary brought up that incident to instigate and escalate a row between he and I . I had helped Gary out tremendously , financially and every other way , and over that last week he tried to sabotage , intimidate and ruin everything I was . The profanity that came out of his mouth angered me deeply . He threatened to stab me . Not to my face , but on the other end of a phone when he was hiding in his mother's house . He was very sneaky about placing himself in the safest areas in the hostel with equally unpleasant little or big bastards . When he wasn't in the Hostel he would be on the phone mouthing off . Threatening to kill and stab me . And when he was in the hostel he would keep his distance and observe your every move . It was infuriating . He was a master of it .

After about 4 days straight of it , I was that worked up , I didn't say anything but we were in the TV room and Victor was like , ' Colum son , com' on , we'll go out for a walk ' . We walked around beside the big fish near the Odyssey and

I said to Victor , ' I'm gona kill this cunt . ' ' C'mon Colum ,
we'll walk back I'll get you a cup of tea . '

As I approached the front door of the Hostel , guess who
walked out with some random meat-head with tattoos .
You guessed it . Gary . My only thought was walking past
him on my way to a cup of tea , but as I passed him he
purposefully bumped my shoulder . It took me one second
to lock on to him and start my onslaught . ' *I'm tellin' ya ,
this ain't hapin' , this ain't hapin' ' ,* he screeched in a
desperate attempt to regain control of the situation . Well ,
if this ain't happening you're in trouble , because this is
exactly what's happening . I had him trapped against the
hostel door . six shots later I was in a momentum .
Uppercuts went in thick and fast . Maybe twelve . For such
a hard man with all his talk . What was coming back was
almost pitiful . It spurred me on 100% . I landed my head
into his mouth and nose at will repeatedly . The snap ,
crackle and pop of my head crunching against his face ,
mouth and cheekbones . Brought me pleasure . I delayed
the pleasure for another day and continued with the job in
hand . Destroying this little bitch cunt . Everything was
working in unison , heads , uppercuts and knees . He
eventually crumbled and whilted . He screamed and
groaned like a girl . Like a little bitch that he was . Like a
little bitch that he has been his whole life . And will be for
the rest of it . He was taller than me . As he crumbled I used
his head to open the Hostel door repeatedly . I was cold
and transfixed on my target . The bloke who was with him
didn't know what to do . Victor gave him a stern look . He
took a step back and observed . I could of opened the door
with his head all day . How dare you say you're going to

stab me . What am I , some little punk from the neighbourhood you can just threaten with a knife . Rosemary came out and came between us . She stuck her hand on my arm . Her gentleness defused the violence . Gary walked off with his tail between his legs . The quick response police were called . Rosemary ran between Gary and I , who was now inside ' His tooth's loose , what was that all about , Colum the police have been called , you don't need this with what you're doing tomorrow . ' I couldn't look her in the eyes . I was still very upset about everything he had said to me . It was what happened to me **several** times before . When somebody can't beat me physically , they mention stabbing me . I take it very personally . The quick response team arrived . I could hear them before I could see them . And when they arrived they thought that I had been beat up , as Gary's blood was on parts of my head . They quickly realized what had gone on and checked the CCTV . One of the officers came up to me . ' Have you done mixed martial arts ? , Where did you learn to fight like that ? ' All I could say repeatedly was , ' He threatened to stab me . ' My grandfather rang him when he heard what had happened and convinced Gary not to press charges . I wasn't alone in thinking he deserved every bit of it and more . Gary went to go and stay with his mummy . That's what these tough guys do when they don't get their own way . Run back to mummy .

It did occur to me that the pleasure was not in the actual act of physical violence but like in a coiled spring . His action released everything that he had put inside me over the past week . The hatred that I had felt of him for five solid days I stored in my body and what happened between us lasted no longer than a minute and a half . I used nothing of my own strength , my own resources . It was all his hatred reflected back on him in the form of a surge of vicious physical violence . There was no other way . Why did he do it ? On some sub conscious level , he might of resented me getting ahead . I had found my way out and was going for it ; he hadn't , but he didn't want to be left behind and so was willing to put himself in a life and death situation to block my progress .

BASIC TRAINING

19 PLATOON

The next day I was due to leave and I gave Victor all the things I was leaving behind : CD player , toaster , kettle , TV , George Foreman . A lot of my uncles and Aunties from my father's side came down to wish me luck and handed me a good luck card with a couple of quid in it . I took a chunk of the money , it could of been £60 , and told my father to deliver flowers , really nice ones , to three or four of the women who had really helped me in that place over the past six months . Rosemary was one of them ; she was such a sweetheart and really accepted and validated some of the things I said when we were having our one on one meetings . So , Thank you Rosemary for being an awesome keyworker and an all round lovely woman . I got a taxi to George Best Airport (although I don't think it was called this yet) . Everything I owned I had with me in my bag .

I rocked up at the Airport and realized I was in the wrong airport . Fuck me , am I ever going to get out of this place? I wondered . George Best didn't fly to Newcastle . I didn't think twice : I got a Taxi to Aldergrove Airport , but I'd missed my flight . With the money from my aunties and uncles I bought myself the soonest one to Newcastle . It was about £80 . It was a relief . I would be a couple of hours late but I would get there and be out of here soon . I'd shaved this morning . Victor said that might go down well . First impressions and all that . I had about two and a half hours to get on the flight . I was pumped . My right hand was damaged from the incident the day before and started to swell . It was full of fluid . I turned my phone off and focused . I was machine-like . Once I get to Newcastle I get a train to Darlington . From Darlington I can get a Taxi to Catterick . I went through it again in my head so there would be no more mishaps . I was almost immobilised until I could stroke each destination off in my head as I got there . I went to the bar and kaned a couple of double Jack Daniels and coke and a couple of Guinness . It settled me slightly , that little bit of drunkenness . It didn't last , and by the time I got to Newcastle , I was sober as a judge again , but I was happy . One down and getting closer to my destination . A few stops and half an hour on the train brought me to Darlington . Two down . I rocked up at Darlington and seen young , fresh-faced blokes everywhere . They all had a similar huge black bag strapped over both shoulders . These went the full length of their backs and even scrapped their arses . I was later to learn that this was issue tissue . Issued kit . I stood there for about half an hour , observing , feeling the vibe assessing this new place for any dangers that might appear . It seemed pleasant and there was a lot of hustle and bustle . Black private taxis were having a field day . Scooping six blokes at a time and whizzing off . I walked to the bus stop just meters away from where the taxis were . None of them looked like British soldiers . They all looked too happy and smiley and young to be British soldiers . It occurred to me : these kids are going through training . I approached a friendly looking young man who looked like he'd help . ' Ya alrite mate , do you know how to get to Catterick ? '

' Yeah , you can jump in with me , ' he said enthusiastically .

The penny dropped : all these kids were going to the same destination - Catterick Infantry School . I jumped in and waited for the taxi to fill up . It was £5 each roughly . He seemed to drive for about fifteen or twenty miles . It was dark . It was probably twelve . When I arrived I saw that they'd put some asshole at the gate ; he was talking to the boys like shit with a big smile on his face . Not letting anyone in the barracks , and a big queue was forming . I tried to explain my case but in the back of my head I was saying , Who is this cunt and where does he get off ? Fucking asshole . He knew what I was thinking and so for whatever reason I went along with starting being polite and respectful even though he was talking to everyone like shit . When I got in the grounds it took me a while to find my block . I was up and down the barracks like a yoyo and didn't relax until I found my floor and my bed space . Cookie , an Lcpl from the Jocks , showed me to my bed space . He was tall and skinny like a beanpole and looked a bit emaciated , really thin and gaunt with short black curly hair and a mild Scottish accent . He was nice to me and explained to the rest of the Irish Guards section that I was sharing a room with them , and to look after me and be nice because I'd just missed my flight and had had a hard time getting here . It was a nice gesture but a bit unnecessary . Within ten or fifteen seconds of me dumping my bag on my bed some big awkward clumsy-looking fucker walked in . He was wearing a Wolves top and had a broad Brummie accent . ' Alright boys , my names Caff and I'm your Section Commander . '

' Yeah well , my names Colum and I'm a Fucking Warrior . '

He went away , and to be honest on first impressions I thought what the fuck is he good for ? He didn't look like he could do anything . How wrong I was . He was all over it . He could do everything . He was fit as a fiddle and with his big long legs he could tab all day . He was an awesome field soldier also . To be honest the years hadn't been kind to him he looked about forty in my opinion and he was a Lsgt . I was shocked when I heard he was a year older than me at twenty-four . Moments after my encounter with Caff I was asked to come in to see the Platoon Sergeant by Cookie . I went in and Davey Walker , my new platoon sergeant , asked me had I been drinking . ' No , No , I haven't , ' I replied . They could probably smell my breath from the couple I had at the airport before . As I was standing there Cookie was correcting my posture physically . It was bizarre . He was saying put your feet closer , put your arms parallel to you your body like this . Put your chest out ... pushing and tweaking my body to the correct position of attention with his hands while I was trying to have this one on one with my full bloke .

I couldn't look Davey Walker in the eye ; I was still really upset about what had happened the day before but I was happy to be here finally . And we weren't alone in the room . There was a room full of people . Davey Walker , Cookie , Caff , Sting , Lsgt Stevie B who talked incessantly about how much of a legend he and his brothers are in their battalion ; then Jack , who I handed a ten-inch banana once from the cookhouse and got an awesome reaction - his response being ' What the fuck is that , is that a dildo ? Get that away from me you weird individual , ' as he stormed off ; and last but not least Mr Dannett , who is the son of Sir Richard Dannett , former Chief of the General Staff . He was an extraordinary bloke . He had more dignity , integrity and character in his spit than most people have in their entire body . It was an honour and a pleasure to meet all these gentlemen , who were all very special in their own way . Immediately , Mr Dannett asked , ' what happened to your hand McGeown ? ' It was bust and it was the size of a bap . I was taken back by his forwardness . I paused and stumbled and looked for the words to try and explain in a humble and dignified way that I was in a fight , that someone who had upset me greatly had got punished for doing so . It all sort of came out back to front , but he got the message . ' It looks broken , go and see a doctor about that tomorrow . ' ' It's not broken sir , It'll be fine in a week . ' Cookie showed me how to ask for my leave to carry on . I did it to Davey Walker . Davey Walker pointed to Mr Dannett and before I could do it again for Mr Dannett he waved me off with a hand gesture : *Go* . I took three steps towards my exit . Davey Walker in his coarse Glaswegian accent , ' McGeown , you're not gona be trouble for us . ' I turned respectfully . ' No Sergeant , ' and walked off to my bed space .

When I got back to my room I'd only been in the block half an hour . I was still pumped , but happy . Final destination stroked off in my mind . The room was twenty metres long and four metres wide . An openly manned ten-bed plus lockers . The carpets looked old and worn and the lockers weren't in great condition . I wasn't friendly . I was doing enough just to pass as approachable and civil . Like in the hostel , I would let who ever wanted to befriend me approach me . It wasn't long . And it was in the size and shape of Dave Kell . He was slightly smaller than me but very stocky and mature-looking , i.e. hairy arms and chest . He wore black glasses with a thick black frame and had a unique Brummie accent . He had black hair and a darker complexion that I was not used to seeing in Belfast . He was half Arabian and half Irish , and a big sweetheart . As he talked to me he immediately put me at ease ; he was non-threatening , warm and friendly . And to this day Dave remains a very dear friend . He loved the Irish . His mother was from Cork before moving over to this side of the UK many years ago . There was Jarvis , another Brummie who again was lovely and into his boxing . He was cheeky and self-contained . He was a pretty boy , and very body beautiful ; everyone took to him instantly . I spent many weekends with Jarvis in Birmingham with him and his family ; he was and still is a dear friend .

Quinlan , where do I start . Jesus , we called him the wiggly worm . He had a little dance when he'd been inspected and when the section commander had his back turned . The dance looked like a wiggly worm and he was always goofing around . He was great craic for all the boys and always lifted the morale . I visited him in Kilburn and immediately took the piss out of him . He lived in a bigger shit hole than I had just come from . He was a good sport and a good soldier .

Siao was the youngest , he was half Chinese , half Scouse . Weird mix , and he was very young . Even with our help he had a hard time in training . He was a good kid , and on one of our first exercises he got the whole section in trouble for leaving a surface-laid shit close to our stag position , in the harbour area . A surface-laid shit is exactly what it says on the tin . In the field ones shit should be buried as far from the harbour area as possible for sanitation reasons . It is possible when on Op's real time to carry your shit with you so as to not leave any trace behind you . In the field this is what's known as ' sign ' . Leaving cigarette butts or wrappers in the field is also sign . It was quite amusing when Caff discovered a shit the size of a log next to the stag position . Lastly there was Neill . He became a dear and devoted friend . He spent some of his life back in Belfast . Really switched on , and , to be honest , knew a bit too much about the way things work in the Army . We eventually found out he had left the Engineers a couple of years before and this was his lifeline , his last crack at a career . He was a dear friend and turned out to be a fine soldier .

And then there was me . I quickly felt a deep connection to the boys . I was the only Irish one in the Irish Guards section so a lot of the other boys in our platoon called me 'Irish' . Original , I know . But you are dealing with a bunch of Infanteers . The first week was all classroom , locker inspections and marching around the barracks getting acquainted to the barracks , facilities , and what conduct was expected of us and what the repercussions were if we fell short . Davey Walker made each of us do an ice-breaker . It's basically where you stand up in front of the rest of the platoon and tell the platoon about yourself for a minute , finished by a joke . When Davey Walker finished his demonstration he told this joke :

' How do you know your girlfriends been drinking tomato juice ? … Because when your fucking her up the arse you have tomato seeds under your foreskin '

Davey Walker was a very funny man . When I stood up , I said , ' My names Colum , I'm from Belfast and I wana go to Iraq and see what it's all about . ' I just said it with honesty and sincerity because I did want to see what all the hype was about . It's part of my nature to want to go to the darkest , dingiest , most dangerous places in my mind and on planet Earth . I think for no other reason than just to say ' I did it ' or ' I was there . ' But more than anything to know inside that you did it or you were there .

My joke was : ' A baby polar bear asks his mummy – Mummy , are you sure I'm not koala bear or a grizzly bear or a panda bear ? ' Mummy says , '' No son , you're a polar bear – go and ask your daddy . '' So the little polar bear jumps off the little ice island and swims over to his daddy . '' Daddy , are you sure I'm not a koala bear , a grizzly bear or a panda bear ? ''and Daddy says , '' No son , you're a polar bear , go and ask your grandma . '' And so the little baby polar bear jumps into the water and swims over to the little ice island his grandma is on . '' Grandma are you sure I'm not a koala bear , a grizzly bear or panda bear '' – '' No son , you're a polar bear , Why'd you ask ? '' And the little baby polar bear replies , '' Cus I'm fffuuucckkking ffreeezzzing! ''

It got a good response . I told it well .

Sometime after our little ice-breaker Neill came up to me , '
You wana see proper war fighting McGeown , proper
soldiering , Afghanistan's the place you wana go , forget
about Iraq . Afghanistan's where it's at . ' I listened and
nodded . The possibility of either Iraq or Afghanistan was
so far away from reality . You have to pass out of training
first and join your battalion before any of this is possible .

We were told about the importance of keeping fit and why
we were gona be pushed extremely hard . Told not to take
drugs and told of the importance health wise on alcohol-
abuse . All basic stuff . But it was a nice week of not doing
too much before the fun started . We were told that the
first six weeks we would be kept in camp . That was sweet
had nowhere to go anyway . We were told stories of
massive physical and moral courage . One such story of
physical/moral courage was told by Mr Dannett during
bayonet training . **I believe** it's more a story of discipline
and bravery . After running us ragged for an hour through
rivers , doing fireman carries , leopard crawls and learning
how to attack straw dummies with a bayonet , he told us a
story about Mount Tumbledown , Falklands . A battalion ,
probably the Jocks , advancing through the battlefield had
taken major casualties and deaths . Amongst the mayhem a
platoon commander grabs a private , he needs a runner .
The private follows suite as he and the commander
advance through the battlefield . The commander is
changing tactics and giving orders as he closes in on fire
positions and bunkers of the enemy . Sections are getting
cut in two and there's no cover . The old hard , fast and
aggressive full-frontal attack is what the commander has
ordered as they slowly take enemy positions . The battle

has been won and both the commander and private are still alive side by side , but the commander notices that the young private has no weapon on him and discovers it had been removed from him in the heat of the battle long ago . ' Why the hell did you come with me when you had no weapon to defend yourself ? '

' I came because you told me Sir . '

Mr Dannett told the story with such passion . ' Guys this is what you might have to do one day . One day you might be that young private , this is why this training is so important . ' He was a great speaker , a classy guy , he would of sounded poetic reading a phone book or a take away menu , but with the content of the story and his passionate voice and energy it was very affecting . Even to me .

He called me into his office one day . ' McGeown you look like you're ready to explode at any moment . '

He was right . My fears and anger with my situation back in Belfast was all bubbling below the surface . That and refusing to ejaculate for the first twelve weeks of basic training , until I was well nested in and had showed everyone ' who's who ' . My fear was not of going back to Belfast , I had too much momentum and couldn't visualize that , but trying to keep a lid on my behaviour was difficult . I needed to progress through this initial stage so a couple of years down the line I might end up in a place worthy of a life . The biggest effort was trying to make myself approachable even though all I wanted to do was fight . It's what my body and mind were tuned to do , and I'd fought so hard to get out of Andytown with my sense of self intact . It was hard to keep dignified , humble and passive when what got me to this stage was innate animal instinct with complete rebellion to what anybody else thought or felt . Never underestimate the strength it takes to be an individual . An individual in the heart of Andytown that says , ' Hello how are you ' in perfect English instead of , *'Alrite mate what's the craic* ' or ' *What's happenin fella* ' in west Belfast slang . Especially when everybody and all your peers in your community are talking that way . To listen to what's inside and conduct yourself on the outside to what your heart says . This takes strength and resolve and courage .

My uniqueness didn't go unnoticed , and was met with resistance from Caff . Every time I was told to drop and do push-ups as a punishment , I showed my exuberance and willingness to participate . I licked the print side of my right thumb quickly , rubbed my hands together animatedly and ecstatically , like my winning horse had just come in , and dropped straight from the vertical position to the horizontal like a falling tree and start banging them out . This little lick of the thumb and rubbing of the hands was a mannerism I took from my uncle ' White lightening ' . Every time after lunch or in the morning just before he picked up his trowel . He would do this little routine . It meant *Let's get down to business* ; I had carried a *Let's go , Bring it on* attitude in Andytown , and it was my deepest intention not to change no matter what . This little mannerism came in handy . The first time I ever did it was when Caff was trying to get his point across with his *correctional training* . My exuberance in taking it cancelled out the *correctional* part , as I was a willing participant . To me it was just training , and after a short while this little mannerism did his head in . With his *correctional training* I became stronger , especially in the eyes of the rest of my section . Couple the push-ups with a big grin as I did it . Mind Games are essential for the survival of basic training because the in-camp stuff is one big head-fuck , if you let it be . If you behave like you don't want something to happen then they'll focus on that and make it happen . Each commander will try and fuck with each individual to either strengthen or test that individual's resolve .

The first time we were ever out in the field we were working in our sections . Sting's section and Caff's section were working together . We were constantly being drilled by Sting . It was all new and he would drill certain things like' Passage of information is everything in this job ' . We were sitting on a bank looking in at Caff . Sting went to one end whispered something and told each person to quietly whisper it to the next guy , passing the message on . It must have been our location because when it got to me Sting said in a questioning tone , ' So! Where are we *then* McGeown '

Just moments before Jarvis had mumbled something into my ear as he was the next bod to me and I couldn't make head nor tail of what he was talking about or what he said . ' What!? ' I replied and instead of repeating it he just shrugged it off and said ' Well that's what *he* said , ' meaning the guy next to him . So when I was asked where we were I said , ' Iraq ' it's all make believe anyway , training for the real thing . Yeah . Fuck it . Iraq . Sting went off on one ' The passage of information is shit here!!! , Fucking McGeown thinks he's in Iraq!!! ' . At this Caff chirped in

' Come here McGowan ' (as he liked to call me) I stood up off the bank , he was on a hill and I was walking up to him . I stood on near as even ground as I could to take away the already large height difference , ' Oi! McGeown what the fuck ' he spoke gently ' Why the fuck d'you say Iraq McGeown ' . ' Oi! McGeown , look at me ' he tightened his hand round my chin strap . The chin strap is the strap attached to your helmet to keep your helmet secure and in place . Two straps run down the sides of both ears . He grabbed one of them and repeated , ' Why d'you say Iraq McGeown ' his voice was still soft but his grip was tightening . I didn't like his hand being this close to my face . I pushed my head down to release his grip ever so slightly . At that he tightened his grip trying to reassert some dominance . I tightened my grip on him , pushing my head down while tightening my neck at the same time rubbing my hard boney forehead against his knuckles . His hand was facing upwards like an uppercut and my forehead was facing horizontal on his knuckles and I was trying to disjoint his grip with the movement and force of my forehead . *Fuck you , you're not gona have control over my head , embarrass me in front of all these boys* .

' Oi! McGowan , what the fuck '

' What the fuck!! ' ………….

' What the fuck are you playing at! '

I was like a Pitbull who wouldn't let go of a football . As he wrestled with my chin strap more aggressively I took a step backwards or forwards to regain my balance continuing my defiant stance . It must of looked quite humourous to the rest of the 2 sections looking in . Eventually he let go and as cool as a cucumber I walked over and joined the section . " I'm not one of these kids that's just left their mummy's tit to be here . You're gona learn all about it Caff " . When I sat down Jarvis was sniggering , ' *You're fucking mad McGowan* . ' I sat there composed . All eyes were on me .

The field in training can be called the area or back area . It's huge and as far as the eye can see it's MOD . Rolling country side . The ranges are flat and long with little protection from the elements . Wind , rain , sun . You sit out in it and wait for your multiple to shoot . If it rains you stick your wet kit on . If it's cold apply warm kit . Sometimes we were told to sit there with our helmets on and apply cam cream for no apparent reason . Caff would give a demand and then count down from 10 and if the demand wasn't completed by every man in the Platoon in the time he would send every man to the flag pole and back .

Forgetting kit on the ranges would also be a flag pole punishable offence . Every range has a flag pole . You fly the flag when there's live firing . Most ranges in training were 600m long . The flag pole is usually located on the 600m mark . You zero your weapon system at 100m and then hit targets at 200m . Mainly 300m and then you bring it back to 400m . A lot of the activity happens at 300m . Repetition . Repetition . Repetition . So when you're sent to the flag pole at 300m . There's a 300m race there . Round it and back . 600m all in . Against the rest of the Platoon . The last ' however many he decided ' would , or ' the first 10

118

wouldn't ' , have to go again . It depends who was trying and who wasn't . If I fucked up then Caff would punish the whole Platoon . Eventually it would just be the whole Irish Guards section . This is what's known as blanket punishment . Inevitably the Platoon or section visited the flag pole on my behalf many times .

I just wasn't used to being treated like a cunt in this way . The Platoon and then the section were a little bit tired of me from this angle . Caff would say' Someone needs to smash McGowan! ' . Making it out that one of my section needed to fill me in . Fill me in into obedience . Firstly all the boys thought I was a real good lad apart from all the flag pole business and I felt the same about each of them . We were all good good friends even if my stubbornness impacted their comfort level . And that's what this blanket punishment is all about . The theory is if the whole section gets punished for 1's misdemeanour . Then the section will either get a grip of this one man . Or . The one man will screw the nut so his section isn't getting beasted for his misdemeanour .

Eventually Caff just sent me to the flag pole . I think he called me over to him . Done that counting down from 10 shit and I rocked up to him on 12 . I was flag poling it for the next hour . Every time he shouted , ' Grenade!!! ' I had to get down and leopard crawl to flag pole . There and back . There and back . There and back . Eventually he called me in . There was grass and mud stains caked all over my combats , especially my elbows and knees . He chin strapped me . I was exerted from my little extra-curricular activity and didn't have the energy to do the ' Pitbull with a football ' routine so instead I used his knuckles as a pillow . I'm always uncomfortable with fists being this close to my face . I caught my breath ' Drink some water McGowan , Get your kit ready you're shooting next ' .

The shit thing about leopard crawling to the flag pole is the admin . You have a limited amount of combats and for the next day your locker has to look exactly the same as everyone else's in the section . So you wash , dry and have clothes presented for the next day as you'll undoubtedly get at least one room and locker inspection . Mix that with the evening and morning duties of swabbing the lines makes it a full day . Runs . Ranges . Tabs . Room and locker inspections . They spring things on you throughout the day **' Pt kit , outside 15 minutes! '** . 50 men have to be outside in Pt kit in 3 ranks . You probably have to clean cam cream off your face and when you get out the whole platoon will be in stretch positions . The boys who were punctual stay in stretch positions . Until every last member of the platoon has left the block . In the hurry you'll forget to lock your locker and when you come back your locker will be tipped out and your bed upside down , ' Security of kit ' is all they have to say .

As brutal as this behaviour or treatment sounds it's essential to desensitizing the boys . This is , I would even say , paramount to the development of a true Infantry soldier . However , I wasn't a boy coming into this system and my life before left me desensitized to pain . Physical . And challenging situations . In many ways the army was like Butlins to me . Wear these clothes . Run , carry this , run with that strapped to your back . Help the guys that lag behind . Here's your three squares a day . A roof over your head . A bit of comfort in a bed and on the last working day of every month there's a wage . Thank you very much . At the end of the day it's soldiering . It isn't beauty therapy . It's going to a foreign land in all weather conditions usually the extremes which is either baltic cold or sizzling hot and having it in you the confidence and the know-how to do the business for up to 6-7 months at a time with a little 2 week R&R break in between .

When we were in the field . I soaked everything in . Skills , drills and tactics . To me it was real time . The bullets were real . The enemy who were usually the sick bods dressed in desert combats and a turban , donated from another platoon , were real . When I was told to hard target I did it like my life depended on it . Hard target is where you present yourself as a hard target to the enemy when leaving a tree line or gate that the enemy could have eyes on . You move fast , low and side to side zig-zagging . Then step into a normal pace of patrolling . If you're not marching , patrolling or taking on enemy then you're taking a knee . Keeping as low profile as possible while you listen to orders . Field life is great .

After about 3 weeks of me not playing ball Caff told our section that he was responsible for personally cutting of the supply to the Iraqi Terrorist Army . Al Queda . Which helped win the war in Iraq . He told us he spent 8 weeks on 8 weeks off in an OP in Iraq . (Observation Post/Point) . Shitting in bags with the Recce Platoon for Battalion . In hindsight it was very unlikely that Caff done any of the above but this was used as a ploy to get the boys to respect

him and his capability and get everyone on side . Until I
heard this I wasn't 100% sold on Caff and his role as section
commander but this little white lie had the desired effect .

In that first 6 weeks Caff kindly demonstrated the correct
way to shave , clean , remove winnots from your arse and
cheese from your knob . As he removed stuff from the
latter two he would put the samples right under some of
the blokes noses so they could appreciate the importance
of it all . *He was thoughtful that way* . When we had locker
inspections each section's lockers had to be identical and
whether it was perfect or not the section commanders
would find fault . Wreck them a bit and then reset an
inspection for an hour later . It was all a ploy to keep us out
of our beds for as long as possible . Keeping us busy . For
the first 6 weeks we were gated . Them 6 weeks we caught
an average of 6 hours sleep a night . We learnt what a pft
was . A personal fitness test . My first one was 9.12 . By the
time I was leaving it was 8.12 . A pft . As many sit ups in 2
min . As many press ups in 2 mins . I averaged about 80
each . And then straight after . A mile and a half run best
effort against the rest of the boys .

The army's amazing . It's like our own little community . It
was safe . I felt safe . In that first 6 weeks they had us in the
corridor every night doing stretch positions . And then they
would give you 10 seconds to run to your room and bring
back a specific piece of kit . Which is impossible for over 50
blokes to achieve that . And then you'd be put into another
stretch position for another 15 minutes . It was fucking
hilarious but after about 6 weeks of it I guess it became a
little mundane . On the weekend of the 6th week I bought

a couple of tickets for Calzaghe v Manfredo . It was in Wales and the army paid for my train . It was about £100 return . Nice one . I flew my brother over and we had a good night out in Wales . I was happy to have the money in my bank to do this . Amir Khan was on the bill as well . It was a good night of boxing but the seats were poor . When I got back I started the next stage of my training and they really pumped up the volume . We started doing boot runs longer distances . Fitness . Fitness . Fitness .

5 years on a building site with real men from an older era , loading , building blocks , working hard in all weather conditions prepared me for life in the field . Although some field exercises it was bitter cold at night and your skin around your neck area would suffer from midgy bites , excessive cam cream use and dirty field sweat . However what I didn't count on is how much damage brand new Army issued boots can do to your feet and heels . Running 8 miles in undulating , rough terrain with 50lb's on your back in ranks of 3 . My heels were raw , skin completely torn off the back of them . This is where zincoxide tape became an infantry man's new best friend . The tape was applied thickly over the raw damaged tissue of the heel . It could stay on for up to a week that's with showers and all . Really durable stuff .

When you've spent a considerable time in the field you get rashes , sweat and spots in places you never did before . The first field exercise I felt bullied . Like Caff was taking advantage , taking the piss . Caff took all our water off us and made us go along time without any . All the while doing attacks , exercises and patrols . In the field 1 day gels into the next , into the next , into the next , until a whole week has gone and you've had little to no sleep , your feet are a mess , you've lost weight , your skin looks less than healthy and the exercise has taken a little bit from you . One of the drills is to change your socks every day . Dead skin from your feet , crossing rivers and sweating can soften skin and erode feet quick time . Talc was instructed to be used but with me this had a negative effect on my feet . It can dry your feet out too much and make it uncomfortable to walk and even make your skin crack which adds to your discomfort levels .

We continued our drill learning . To me it was ridiculous . I didn't see the point . It didn't make a difference . You had to do it and you had to do it to the best of your ability . Correctly . It was really difficult to loosen up to drill . They wanted you to push your chest out and raise your chin unusually high . If you did that in Andytown you'd be knocked out quickly . It took me a while but I got the hang of it . I quickly noticed that there was 2 types of soldier . One for the drill and one for the field . I knew which one I was but observed that many people compensated with good drill that were lacking in other areas . Well I was a killer not a driller . To be honest I hated my time on the drill square . It seemed like a waste of valuable training time . And I hated bulling my boots . To this day I'm useless at bulling boots . I used to pay and do favours for someone else to do my boots . Even when I got to battalion I paid my roommate £30-£40 a month just to keep my boots in good nick . Thanks Charlie .

Before I left the hostel Victor had told me to put £300 on

Kauto Star to win the Cheltenham Gold Cup . I trusted him that much I instantly did it and in the 7th week of training my bet came in . Kauto Star won the race of his life . Such a strong competitive horse and must rank up there with the best Steeple Chase horses of all time . I got £650 from my slip and that weekend went into Darlington and threw £200 in Victors bank account . I Thanked him for the Tip and told him to have a drink on me . There is a saying I heard in and around my time in the Hostel . I might of read it in a book and it was , ' *In Life you only need validated from the one , right person* ' . Well Victor was that person for me . He was the cheapest best life coach I ever had or could ever of wished to have and was imperative and absolutely supportive and influential in the direction I went . When I ever mentioned the Army he simply said , ' McGoo Go for it , If I was your age I'd do it myself , I'd of been fit to , what is there here for you ' .

Davey Walker was moved like a piece of chess to another Platoon .

We all really liked him . He was great craic and a real character . Langy came in as our new Platoon bloke . Langy is a 6ft 4 Geordie with a huge chest and massive shoulders . Big , strong , powerful looking man but very humble about it . After a week of settling in he called me into his office , ' I don't know what it is about you McGowan , Where you're from , I've been watching you cutting around , It's not normal , All I ever hear in this office is your name . McGowan this , McGowan that , sometimes fuckin' bastard 6 times a day ' . When I was standing to attention at the other side of his desk I noticed a little framed picture of

Langy that he'd brought with him . It sat on his desk . In it he was wearing a blue beret and looked early 20's at the time . He didn't get big over-night . He was a big fucker back then and all . ' You're good on the stretcher McGowan , that's because you've got aggression , you'll need that , it's in-camp were you need to work ' . ' Let's see if you can go a whole week without being mentioned in here ' he held a moment were we both understood each other . Of course I couldn't . Who was he kidding . Sound as Langy was . Some stranger with a Rank slide , giving him full possession of my soul . Forget about it .

Langy loved having craic with me . I think he was drawn to me . I was raw , wild and unpolished . He knew my nature . They all knew my story . Coming into the office first day smelling of drink with a bust hand . We were on the ranges one day ,' *Fuckin' Andystown* McGowan – I've been involved in some riots up there ' he had a look on his face that suggested that these riots were quite tasty . ' We were always up for it though ' , I replied . ' You think you'd have me McGowan ' , I knew what he meant but I did the necessaries ' Have you ' , I replied .

Caff was looking in . He was my section commander and his role was as a choke chain for his Pitbull that he had in the section . Me . Caff , ' That's have you Sir . Oi! McGowan Sir! – Respect the Rank McGowan ' . If I had a pound for every time I heard the term , ' Respect the Rank ' , I'd of been sitting on a senior G-mans wage not a trainee Guardsman's . Caff and Mr Dannett were looking in . I was sitting down waiting for my multiple to be called . Langy was standing imperial , tall , big and proud . ' Yes McGowan . Have me .

D'you think you'd knock us out ' . He asked me in a tone that demanded an honest answer .' Yeah ' . Forget the Sir . When the conversations going this direction this big guy ain't getting an inch of me . No advantages . Mr Dannett was looking in with a massive grin , his grin looked insaciable , like a kid looking down at the foot of a Christmas tree on Christmas morning with everything he'd asked for, looking at me like all his Christmases had come at once .

With every one of my responses to Langy his grin grew even more . Maybe not believing what was coming out of this 5ft10 wiry kid to this 6ft4 mountain of a man . Or maybe because I talked with such authority and that I believed in myself that much . That might have been what brought the smile to his face . ' Could you knock us out in three punches McGowan ' . We were still in the moment and with an honest view of myself coming head to head with a man that size I replied , ' Yeah ' my jaw was protruding squarely .

In Andytown such conversations don't get to this stage before shots are thrown and landed . But still this honesty flowed between he and I . My brow was frowned . I showed him the whites of my eyes to let him know that I was not exactly relishing this conversation . ' Could you knock us out in two punches McGowan ' his pitch became more desperate as he was playing in on this role of a hapless victim , put on of course . Same tone ' Yeah ' . I was steady and calm , the mood was jovial but we were talking seriously about a serious thing , ' *Fuck me McGowan!* – One punch ' in one last gasp from his pretend hapless victim role

. ' No Sir , But I'd *sting ya*' , I gave him that respect . He had a head the size and shape of a concrete block . Maybe it would take a couple to down this bear of a man . Mr Dannett walked away smile still on his face . ' I'm Gona Fuckin' knock you out McGowan' he took 3 large steps over and slowly grabbed a tuft of my smock under my chin with his huge right hand . He closed his huge hand around the contents in it and held his left fist in front of my head as he roared in a geordie accent that'd been polished year by year working with and instructing officers , **' Look at my hands McGowan – They're the size of your head! '** . His fist touched my nose and blocked out the sky . They weren't the size of my head . About ¾ the size of my head . He used to say , ' This trainings designed so when you see your target in Iraq or Afghanistan or whatever bastard place they send you . You don't think twice . You fuckin' drop your target ' . He would demonstrate by putting an imaginary rifle in his shoulder and then by pulling an imaginary trigger .

Langy was a star . A great guy . A great character . He was very patient with me .

Mr Dannett returned to Battalion to be deployed on Herrick 1 . Afghanistan . And knowing what I know of his character he was playing a lot more than just a back stage role . He had a lead by the front and by example mentality and quite honestly he's one of the finest gentlemen I've ever had the honour of meeting .

When on the ranges you're exposed to the elements and to subsidize that you're offered a scoff bag and a couple of norgis(large 2 gallon olive-green flasks) filled with tea and coffee . The scoff bag usually has an apple , a cheap sausage roll or pasty , could have a sandwich instead of the pasty or sausage roll , a packet of crisps , an orange Club biscuit . If you're really lucky you'll get a Mars bar . The coffee's alright if you're cold . But the tea tastes like Bangladesh dish water . Weak , tasteless . Myself having more of a swimmers and boxers build there isn't much natural fat on me . So when I'm not moving , and static I felt the heat leave me quite quickly . I compensated that by drinking cups and cups of warm coffee . As I walked to my lane with my kit on to take my shoot . My sudden movement triggered me needing to release fluid from my bladder . I didn't wana bitch and moan and hold the shoot up so I thought I'd hold it in . After my first 10 shots we had a break . I initially said , ' Sergeant I need to take a piss I've drunk to much coffee . Can I go over there ' , I pointed to a bush that ran the length of the range . He blanked me and shouted to the detail on the range , ' Alright fellas get ready for the next shoot ' . It was Lsgt Stevie B , ' Listen Sergeant if I don't go over to that bush now I'm gona piss myself ' . I put my weapon system down with the muzzle facing down the range and I took two or three steps in the direction of the bush . Stevie B **, ' McGowan!!! Do not leave the range when your weapon is Live and there's shooting taking place '** , he shouted with authority . Now I had his attention . ' Sergeant I'm telling ya' if I don't go over there **now** I'm gona piss myself ' , I looked at him like it's *your* choice . He had a resounded look on his face like I was speaking a foreign language . One of which he had no interest for . ' Ok then I'm pissing myself ' . It was warm and flowed heavy . I stood there looking at him with my palms facing the sky and filled my boots . ¾ of a pint of piss went down my left leg . I tried to shake most of it out as it hit my boots . Stevie B was laughing , ' *Awesome* ' he walked away with a grin on his face ' *Fucking Awesome* ' . Caff came over ' What's this . Did you Piss yourself McGowan ' . We shared a moment . I gave him a cheeky little pout as I nodded my head . '' It's sweet isn't it '' etched all over my face . I carried on with the shoot . From that day on I never drank coffee on the range . Lesson learnt .

In camp the section commanders take it a turn at a time to stay with the boys at night . It only takes one section commander to take charge of a platoon and keep the boys out of their beds at night . The section commanders work it in rotations . Caff's specialty was water parades . He would get the whole platoon out . The length of the corridor and play the song '' I would walk 500 miles '' from the Proclaimers and on the chorus you would have to down your litre of water . You would have to put your left foot forward and do a little jig . Thrusting forward with your hips . Everybody doing this at the same time and necking their water was great craic . When you were done you'd have to hold your army issued water bottle over your head upside down to show you'd finished . If you had any left you'd have to fill the whole thing up again and start over . It was best to do your litre first time around . Some section commanders give you an hour of Phis in the evening in the corridor . Stretch positions or doing physical exercise with your gas mask on . Sometimes they mixed it all together . Water parade followed by stretch positions . Exercises like star jumps and burpee's with the gas masks on . Some people threw up in their gas masks . Haha!! Lovely . Then they were excused .

Each section commander gets control of his section one way or another . The first 8 weeks or so Caff would constantly be saying , ' Fucking Standby Men!! ' . It was in a not so sure of himself tone . ' Fucking Standby! ' , it was some sort of warning but it wasn't there yet . It wasn't having the desired effect . I didn't know what this was . I really really didn't . I know if you're a television you can be put in standby but how does a person standby . Every time he said it . I was so confused . It seemed like such an empty and vacant thing to say to the boys that I didn't take much notice of it but as the weeks progressed he turned , ' Fucking Standby Men! ' into a bit of a threat . Like you are going to receive punishment if this doesn't happen . Example . ' If the swabbing's not done Fucking Standby Men! ' . Initially with the boys when he wanted a cigarette he'd say , ' Who's got a fag ' that evolved to , ' Fag me ' which evolved to , ' Regal ' specifying the particular and only cigarette that would quench his thirst or else it's a beasting for the section . Which evolved to him simply holding up his 2 fingers and counting down from 10 .

Around the 12 week mark we got that bored in the evening if we had spare time we would have little one on one boxing matches . I would promote , instigate and encourage the boys to box each other at night to get the craic going in the lines . It was awesome fun and all the boys who took part loved it . I had a pair of mitts and a pair of 12oz gloves I'd packed with me . I would give the mitts to the slightly weaker if there was one . You can punch harder with them . Jarvis and Quinlan got matched up and in the middle of the contest Quinlan done the wiggly worm dance .

Showboating . He soon realized there was a time and a place for the wiggly worm . Jarvis started cuffing him around the head from every direction . This new dance could of been called ' Knocked around ' . Quinlan tried to gain composure but it was too late . Jarvis had momentum and I had to break it up . Jarvis the winner by TKO .

THE MARS BARS ARE ON ME

As time went by my reluctance to completely surrender myself and leave myself open to what the training team wanted to do with me became apparent . They became incredibly vexed at my stubbornness and sometimes couldn't help themselves from laughing at it . In front of me . Lcpl Cook . Cookie . Had stored our unused Mars bars from the scoff bags . The ones that for whatever reason we never received . From the ranges . Cookie was like a little squirrel who was gathering his chestnuts for the hard times . He stored them neatly in his own little private one man room . He had them stacked solid . In the vegetable drawer at the bottom of his fridge . I could see that he held this little collection of Mars bars close to his heart . But I did decide that they belonged to us and so one weekend when he was not in the block . I made my way to his fridge . I took them out . Went out to the lines and proceeded to hand them out . Handing some people 3 at a time until they were all gone . They were ours anyway . However when Caff found out about this he did not share the same opinion and he told Dave Kell , ' Tell Mcgowan to get in here and bring me some scoff ' . I walked in eating a Mars bar . He was sitting down with his head facing the ground polishing his boots and before he locked eyes on me he said ' Oi! Mcgowan whats this I hear about you stealing Mars bars on Cookie (Lcpl Cook) ' . ' *I don't know what you mean Sergeant* ' . As I took a full bite of the Mars bar in my hand and looked him square in the eye . **' Oi !!!! Mcgowan what the fuck!!! Are you taking the piss!! Take that fucking Mars bar out of your mouth . I'll fucking smash you , ya' little crow** (Combat Recruit Of War)' **' Fucking Stand to attention '** . As I stood to attention I coolly dropped the piece of Mars bar from my mouth to my hand all in one sharp , smooth motion . It fell from my mouth to my left hand as I was stood to attention . Stevie B was in the room and he couldn't control himself . His big hand covered his face . I seen him smile and shake his head beneath his hand. Trying to mask his reaction to the humour that was going on . The dynamic between ballsy trainee Guardsman and angry section commander . Caff WAS angry . ' May I have your leave to carry on Sergeant please '

' Fuck off '

I can't remember what my punishment was for that mars bar incident . I was always at something through training . I couldn't help myself . With all the discipline and structure I was just trying to stay alive inside and hold on to my sense of self . At any cost . On the way to the cookhouse every day I would pass this little road kill . It was a hedgehog . Every progressive day it looked worse . One day I decided to scoop it up with a couple of big leaves and place it in Siao's locker for a laugh . Siao's bedspace was right next to mine and if it was removed when having a room and locker inspection one day it would have been great craic . When I placed it in I couldn't contain myself . I was like a naughty kid and as soon as Siao walked into the room after coming back from scoff he sensed that there was something up . ' *What the fuc' la , what the fuck have you done to my bed space ya jac' cunts '.'* Nothing ' , I replied . Dave Kell was in on it . He'd seen me do it . I'd stuck this dead little patriot right at the back of his shelve behind his pt shorts . He twigged on straight away and when he removed it . He jumped . He was mortified . I thought I'd get someone else with that little stunt . So I wrapped it in newspapers and stuck it outside Cookie's room . Needless to say it didn't go down too well and I was back squadded to 21 Platoon . Which meant I had to repeat the last 4 weeks I had already done with this new platoon before passing out of training .

In fact it was the icing on the cake . My stubbornness and willingness to do things my own way had created a situation where they'd made it very easy to back squad me . Caff would threaten me at times when my behaviour was at its worst , ' Fucking 21 Platoon for you McGowan , you keep it up! ' . *' No dramas Sergeant , I'll show them how it's done! '* . Especially with the Mars bar situation and then there was an incident that I wasn't going to mention . But here goes . Every section commander in 19 Platoon took pleasure in wrecking my room and locker and tipping my bed and bed space . One time they emptied my box of Daz washing powder over the contents of my locker and my bed . They wanted me to snap , break , React . I just smiled but they'd done it once too often . The reason I stayed in 19 Platoon so long was my supreme physical fitness and as I was out doing the Steeple Chase of which I came second . Pushing myself to unusually deeper levels ,entering harder places within myself , basically blowing out my arse hole . One of the Section commanders sneaked round to my bed space and it was turned upside down for my arrival back .You can wreck my room all you want but I didn't respect the timing of this one . Expect a guy to put his heart and soul into something like a Steeple Chase and at the same time while he's blowing out his arse . Sucking in air from the next town over . A tipped bed space is his reward . So I went into their little room that night and didn't exactly wreck it but took what was hanging on the rails and fucked it on the ground . Payback – Yeah! . But my cards where marked from that day on . They never questioned me about it . But they all knew it was me . Like I said . The dead hedgehog was just the icing . This might look bad on me wrecking a section commanders locker . We were at the 16/17 week mark and I'd been putting my body through serious trauma every day . It was so unexpected and so undeserved that it was my natural reaction to do this . I was coming first or second in Pft's , Steeple chases , pushing myself , putting my body under immense stress . I'd earned the right for the section commanders to leave my locker alone . Whether I locked it or not . To be fair a very strong proud Welsh kid by the name of Nicholas always beat me by a couple of seconds on the pft . The Irish and Welsh are a lot in common . Both strong and proud people . The point is I was pushing my heart and lungs to extreme exertion every day and they're little statement . Was like a cream and custard pie to my face . For my efforts .

When you push yourself to physical exertion your body releases endorphins that make you feel good . If you're in tune with your body . You can control this feel good flow into your body . For all the physical exercises I was doing I never once treated myself to any of these endorphins until this Steeple Chase . Until this Steeple chase I never left my real comfort zone . The tape that holds my helmet straps in place loosened up . And especially the last 500m was increasingly painful . The hard helmet would bounce with every stride and knock 60-70 times per minute on the top of my cranium as I ran . The stress of having to control that pain because I wasn't going to give up second place and more importantly I was still fighting for first . Controlling my breathing . Lactic acid build up . Remaining focused . By the time I got to the end I was that relieved I gave myself a nice hit of endorphins . What this does is make your body feel pleasure and leaves you open because the pleasure puts your guard down and when I saw what they had did to my locker and bed space . I was for a moment sensitive to their bullshit and so reacted . My reaction to their locker got me even and then my shield went up for the duration .

3 days into 21 Platoon I repeated the Steeple Chase . Its 2.8 k of running through a course with helmet and boots on , running through water up to your waist over things under things at certain intervals they make you crawl distances . I came second . I was happy enough with that . Like in 19 Platoon I always came second in the pft . But this time in 21 Platoon it was to Knocker . Who had unusually long legs like a giraffe . He'd always beat me by just a couple of seconds . Sometimes 2 . You stick me on a stretcher though and I more than carry my own weight . I can run with that fucker all day . 21 Platoon was much more relaxed than 19 Platoon and at first I enjoyed the relaxed atmosphere . They seemed to finish early at around 5 . And have the rest of the day to sort out their admin .

EXTRA TRAINING

21 PLATOON

We practiced the 12ft wall again and again . It's part of the obstacle course . And a section can win or lose all on the 12ft wall . The section commanders are fiercely competitive when it comes to their own section . Regimental pride is at stake and if a section is weaker than another it gets ripped by the opposing section commanders because the people joining your regiment are your regiment .

It's this regimental pride that turns grotty , clueless civilians into butterflies . In infantry terms butterflies are squared away professional soldiers . The transformation can be remarkable . This regimental pride had Mitchell my new section commander in 21 Platoon . Standing over us for 45 minutes while we practiced the 12ft wall over and over and over again . I'm one of the last ones to go over so my initial job is to heave blokes up . They stand on my cupped hands . The reason my hands are cupped and fingers not interlocked . A couple of boy's fingers have broken in the past when they heaved men up with interlocking fingers . They're cupped . Between my groin . I'm in the squat position , back against the wall . They run towards me to power themselves up . They stand on my cupped hands I heave them up . The other foot hits my shoulder and as their fingers hit the top of the wall they grab hold . I turn and push their feet upward . As they tighten their leg against the pressure of my pushing hand . It's a forceful step , up and over . The tallest of the section will be left last . They'll jump from the ground . The second and third last men are on the top of the wall , they pull him up , place his hands on the wall and jerk him up , up , up and over and then jump down themselves and continue with the rest of the course . We got the time of this . For the whole section over the 12ft wall to just over a minute and my hands and forearms were a bit fucked by all these fully grown men using me as a stepping ladder . So Mitchell was happy with the practice after the 45 minutes . And we all called time .

The big day for the obstacle course . Hence , the 12ft wall real time , arrived . And like I said regimental pride was at stake .

Everything went smoothly . Right up until the last man . Kaka . A crazy big Fijian with biceps the size of helium balloons . And I did wonder if there was helium in his biceps because his arm strength was shite . His inability and lack of desire to pull himself up was clear from the start . As he jumped we grabbed him . The next step was to pull him up , place his hands on the wall and assist him as he pulled himself up with his own strength . Kaka had other plans . I think he thought " Fuck it I'll let these two on top of the wall do all the work " . And a lot of the times he had no vision of where the top of the wall was and seemed rather uninterested . It was incredibly frustrating because not only did he not have the strength and desire to pull his own weight but when we grabbed hold of his arms or hands his weight was dead and nearly pulled us off the top of the wall . When we did have a good tuft of his hand or arm he started walking up the wall like he was Spiderman or even better you know that old Batman and Robin series from years ago when their walking up the side of a building and their capes are still flat . That's what he was doing . Sooner or later you hit as high as you can go and because your actually walking a couple of feet **out** from the wall . Not only are you nearly pulling the people of the top of it . But you only hit a certain height before you inevitably fail . Poor Kaka he wasn't the cleverest tool in the box . My Northern Irish accent telling him what to do . And his Fijian selective hearing . There was a bit of a language barrier . Time was ticking . We were losing and I was looking at him like , " You can't be this fucking thick , You're taking the piss " . Two more attempts in the Batman and Robin fashion had me in fits . Uncontrollable fits of laughter . It weakened me which made it near impossible to even pursue the possibility of Kaka getting over the 12ft wall .We abandoned it and went round carrying on with the obstacle course . It was the only time in training I laughed uncontrollably . All the comedic ingredients mixed together pushed my buttons . 2 minutes on and the laughs were all gone . It was back to business as we powered through the rest of the obstacle course as a section .

In the evenings I found myself more and more just running up to the gym with my boxing gloves and punching the bag for 10 - 15 minutes just to burn of a bit of energy and tension . Some of the section commanders from my new platoon spied me . They were in lifting free weights when I was hitting the bag one day . It was Gibbo and Mitchell . My new section commander . But it was Gibbo who called to me as I walked past the weights room on my way out of the gym . ' Young man when you join the Irish Guards you should go for the battalion boxing team . As a boxer myself I had 17 wins and 3 defeats ' . It was a huge compliment . ' Thank you Sergeant ' . I walked off quite happy with the thought that 1 day I might actually get to leave this place and join the Irish Guards boxing team . Over the coming weeks I repeated alot of the field exercises that I had already done with 19 Platoon . I enjoyed it . Digging trenches , working round the clock - not getting any sleep , doing attacks and getting bugged out from harbour areas was fun and I enjoyed the unpredictability and excitement of it all .

At the 18 week point with 21 Platoon we got a long weekend and were instructed to make the most of it as it was the last real break we would be getting before we passed out so I went back to Belfast . The devil you know . Right . I know I'd left with the intention of never going back but I'd been in the army for 22 weeks now in total because of my back squadding . I went back to Andytown and was looking to stay in my fathers or aunt Janet's . My father opened his door to me but true to form no such thing as a free bed and breakfast . He got his ladder out and made me jump on his roof and scrape the moss of his clay roof tiles with a wall paper scraper . Back and front of the roof . His neighbour came out . An elderly woman and at this my father relishing his role of boss or foreman , ' Don't worry Miss Fitzgearld I'll get him to do your roof as well ' . " *Fuck ! Cheers Da , You want me to do the whole fucking street* " . I was then made scrape all the stuff out of his guttering and the neighbours . The neighbour was a part of the semi detatched property but what really pissed me off was that he made me wear a baseball cap as I did it . In case anyone recognized me as I was now a British soldier and all that .

He has good reasons to be paranoid . My father lived through the Troubles and some of his friends have been killed . Murdered . He told me that his best mate Fitzy once avoided being picked up in a black taxi by the Shankill butchers on the Antrim road . It was 5 o clock in the morning and Fitzy was leaving a girlfriend home . A black taxi full of people turned around from the other side of the road and came back towards him . Fitzy shit himself . Ran into some street and hid under a car . He once explained it to me that there were two types of faction groups within the Nationalionst movement when he was a very young man . There was the ' Doves ' who wanted to do things peacefully and then there was what he described as the ' Gun ' who were the diehard nationalists who were willing to kill and try to make the change with force . And in the Nationalist community between these two there was that much in-fighting between them that it was a very dangerous time to voice an opinion or make publicly your stance . There was a lot of in-fighting in the nationalist community at the end of 75 and in the 80's and when these republican feuds were going on there was more killed in this in-fighting than by or with the opposing Loyalist groups . Extreme Nationalists being those who were willing to fight , kill or be killed for a United Ireland . Extreme Loyalists willing to do the same for the North to remain part of Great Britain .

Even in my lifetime in 1998 when my father was driving to Glenavy on his way to a meal with my mother . He was the first on the scene of a murder that had just taken place . An innocent catholic taxi driver by the name of John McColgan was the murder victim . Initially my father thought it was a drunk who'd stumbled into the middle of the road or worst case senario . A hit and run . There's a pub at the top of the Hannahstown Hill called the Lamh Dearg . I know the Lamh Dearg very well . They have a GAA team and the pitch resides just next to the club . I've played many times on this pitch . Sometimes out of my skin and directly adjacent to the Lamh Dearg is Pryor's scrap yard . I spent many hours in this scrap yard looking for parts for my Pug 106 when I had it . A doorman once put his fist through my driver's side window which sprayed a shower of paned glass all over me and my lap . I was sitting in the driver's seat at the time . Pryor's would have been used to purchase a new driver side window . Everyone with a car in West Belfast knows Pryor's scrapyard . John McColgan wasn't a hit and run or a drunk who'd stumbled onto the middle of the road on his way back from the Lamh Dearg . He was killed by the LVF . Shot at point blank range 5 times in the back of the head . The killers jumped into his taxi at a taxi depot opposite the Whitefort Inn on the Andytown road . When John McColgan reached half way up the Hannahstown Hill going towards the Lamh Dearg . The killers must of said , ' *Here boss stop the taxi here for a second* ' . Either way the taxi was brought to a halt and John McColgan , husband and father of 2 was executed . His only crime was that he was catholic . My father said his face was swelled and protruding a couple of inches from his face as he was breathing his last breaths and on closer inspection he realized that he was not a hit and run and had in fact been shot . My father said that the murderers had tucked his arms under his oxters and dragged him to the middle of the Hannahstown Road in this position before making the getaway in his taxi . His arms were under his oxters when my father came across him . Confirmation of the name on his name tag which was attached to his waist belt confirmed him as John McColgan . My father knew him and had fixed his car before . Being a local mechanic . When the police arrived my father gave a full description of his car as it was not on the scene and missing . He told the police that it had not passed him so must of went the direction of the Lamh Dearg . Out towards the countryside . My father parked his car across the middle of the road so no one would run over Johns Body and ruin the crime scene . My father was saddened by this event .

After a couple of days back from basic training and under my fathers' routine . I'd had enough and spent the duration of my break with my aunt Janet . Being with my father under his roof had brought up feelings of old . Feelings that were a little hurtful and far from pleasant . So after an unrelaxing break in Belfast . I came back to complete the rest of my basic training .

With 3 weeks to go came the big one . Final Ex . It lasts a whole week out in the field with everything that we had done before . Compounded into one week . Sleep depriviation , building and manning OP's , attacks , holding positions , stagging on . All of this occurring 24hrs round the clock . After that . 1 week of live firing in Warcop and then a week of drill . To practice the pass out parade and then Pass out parade will fall on the Friday . But first there was a big , long , gruelling exercise in front of us . On final

144

ex we were kept low on information . That's the way some of these exercises are . You're given little bits of information but to keep the element of surprise is essential . We packed our bergens . We had mountains of shit to carry . Enough food and ammo for a week , picks , shovels , spare boots , clothes , socks , warm kit , wet kit . When it came to stuff that the section had to carry me being me I volunteered to carry a lot of it . My bergen was full and heavy . SAS style .

Then the ammo came out . Mitchell came over to me . In front of the rest of the section commanders .' I want you to carry link ' . I didn't have a machine gun but link is so heavy that it is unfair for just the gunners to carry their own ammo by themselves . Link is fed through the guns and is weighty were a rifle takes magazines which are much lighter. Link is not like food or clothes . It's concentrated weight which can't be manipulated or packed to spread throughout the bergen . When you tab with excessive amounts of link you feel it . It's like tabbing with rocks in your bergen , ' Yeah sure' , I was very nonchalant and cool about it . Giving an aire of " I can do anything you have in stall for me so crack on chief " . He handed me it was either 800 or a thousand link . The rest of the section commanders were looking in at this point . He was challenging my manhood . ' Yeah I'll pick it up in a minute ' . Word got around from some of Mitchell's blue eyed boy's . His favourites . I wasn't 1 of them . Nor did I wana be . I was coming to his battalion and he didn't like me . I suspect he thought I was cocky . Of course . I was cocky . But I could back it all up massively . So Oggy his blue eyed boy opened his mouth , ' *Yeah Mcgowan Mitchell says he's gona break you* ' . ' Is that right ' , I looked at Oggy , his blue eyed boy , as if Fuck off and stop being a pest .

My bergen was 1 heavy motherfucker . The heaviest on that exercise bar none . It was an insurgence tab to our first harbour area . We didn't know how far it was and in what direction . It turned out to be 12 miles of paths and mountains . After 5 miles I was in shit state . Every step I took strained my body . I could feel some of my abdominal organs strain with each step as I carried the weight and pushed forward . It felt like each organ was working individually and not as a complete engine . At that moment I was suffering . Physically . I was determined to make it to that harbour area to fuck that baldy cunt off . Mitchell . I started the tab and exercise in good spirits but to see boys who weren't even in the same league as me breezing it while I was struggling like a whore in heat fucking broke me . People were passing me and in the distance I could see that they had stopped at their first RV . Rendezvous point . Basically a pit stop . I was 50m behind the last man in my section and trailing . Normal spacing's are 10m and I was 700m from the RV which was in the distance . The RV was at the top of a steady gradient . The first section and half of Mitchell's section were already in . The RV was under a large lone tree and it sat at the peak of the gradient .

I could see Mitchell looking down with a big grin on his face . Williams the first man from the last section was in on the plot when it came to the link I was carrying and he easily gained ground on me . As he passed me ' McGeown just dump the link and stop being so proud ' , he said in his Welsh accent. He helped me decide . I walked another 200m towards our RV and 200m away from it . I dropped my bergen . It fell like a boulder and I proceeded to empty what might of been 500 link onto the side of the road . As I approached the RV Mitchell said in an animated and self-assured way , ' That's just made my exercise , no matter what else happens on this exercise that's my highlight , seeing you like that ' . So I said in an equally animated and self-assured voice ' Well Thank you , if it made you smile it was all worth it ' . I went in , got into my position . Sat down for 2 minutes before we stepped off again .

My bergen was much lighter . I could feel the difference . But it was still a heavy motherfucker . Another 7 miles later and a series of moaning and groaning from the boys up and over mountains finally to our harbour area . We weren't but settled when we were told to start digging our fox holes . And dig we did . We did a series of attacks and exercises that I literally can't and don't want to remember . But it was gruelling and relentless . After a week of field life at its very roughest we had a well deserved rest at Warcop before starting live firing . Live Ranges . When we were in the barn-hut in 3 sides of a square cleaning our weapons just after final Ex Roy . A Lsgt and section commander of the jocks came in . He looked pleased with *himself* that **we** had all completed Final Ex . He looked well rested and fully fed and hydrated . As he stood in front of the 3 sides of the square he proceeded to ask a bone question to each of the boys 1 by 1 . The question was 'If you had to fight anybody here who do you think no matter what you did you wouldn't beat them ' . The question was directed at the group purely for me . I knew it . He was standing there in full physical health and I was sitting there genuinely in the worst physical nick I'd ever been in in my life and still the worst I've ever been in . To this very day . A couple of people mentioned my name . I was embarrassed . And when it came to me my frustration of being trapped , forced to sit down , told to clean my weapon and then forced to answer a stupid question bubbled to the surface and Roy received an honest answer , not by a trainee guardsman but by a young man who had conquered his demons and was determined that this Lsgt wasn't going to merely assert or talk himself into pole position like *he'd* earned the right to ask me such as question , ' I'd smash anyone , including you's 2 ' , as I looked Mitchell and Roy in the eye . Before he could say a word I continued , ' Why , Are you terribly upset by that ' . Mitchell sat there quiet and looked at the floor but Roy had other ideas .

Roy , ' Terribly upset , What'd you mean... terribly upset ' , he squabbled

' Well there's upset and there's terribly upset , Are you terribly upset ' , questioning his emotional state , at my answer .

Roy covered the distance between he and I quite quickly . I was still sitting down , ' I've had enough of this ' . Maybe it was the week of trauma to my body but I didn't react quickly . I only woke up as a big left hook connected to my temple . It might of resembled Only fools and Horses when Del-boy falls through the bar standing up as I myself fell over **still** in the sitting down position . Roy was short and stocky , very muscular , powerful and strong . He was a fully fledged man , very fit and strong . He proceeded to punch me in the head , shoulders , arms and ribs as I blocked and parried what I could in a tight defence with my back flat on the barn floor and my hands cupping my head with my elbows rolling side to side to protect my body and ribs . My body felt empty and depleted of nutrients after the weeks exertion and shenanigans but my pride and heart had not been dented . I was on the ground and he was over me . He was hitting me some good , damaging blows and I could feel their affect as they landed . He was caving me in with his big plodding shots and when he thought I was done he jumped up . It was 20-30 seconds . What I said about Roy is absolutely true . He was strong and powerful and had a good physique . He also had a bit of a Van Damme complex about the way he carried himself . In mannerisms . And he was completely in love with himself . His own biggest fan . Mars bar and eat himself spring to mind if I think about Roy . He went into the center of the 3 sided square . You could of heard a pin drop . He proceeded to try and orchestrate the boys who I imagine didn't know what to do **. ' IS THAT IT !!! IS THAT ALL !!! '** , he roared in a broad Glaswegian accent . *" This fuckers been watching to many Gladiator and Troy movies . This fucker thinks it's over "* . I got up unassuming not looking him in the eye and walked towards open space out of the barn about 10m away from him . I stopped and looked at him from the side on , took my top off and said ' Let's go ' . He was willing if not surprised and came right for me . We locked arms and initially I could feel that he was stronger than me . He had me in such a way that I couldn't throw a punch and if I could the only thing he was giving me was his body . Not good enough . If I let go . I'm coming straight across his jaw . We waltzed and moved and wrestled . Knowing that I had only 3 or 4 clean effective damaging punches in me . As we were head to head still fighting for supremacy of each other . The thought in my heart was saying . " You're gona have to fucking kill me , You're gona have to fucking kill me " . Over and over and over again . He realized that I was gearing up for 1 big shot across his jaw . Held me tight . Then pushed me away , walking away at the same time , **' Get him away from me! '** as he walked away hurriedly , towards the training staff house . I was angry at the way he did business.

' Yeah! You're a good one , Why didn't you ask me out ? , You wait til I'm sitting down cleaning my weapon ... Ya Fucking fanny!! '

I went back to my seat to continue cleaning my weapon . My rifle parts were everywhere . I picked up my gas parts and brought them to Mitchell so he could inspect them . I handed them to him . Before he could say anything I asked him ' Was that honorable ' . He told me to Fuck Off and he handed me my parts back . I went back to my seat and sat down like nothing happened and tried to continue cleaning my parts . ' Fuck this ' , I got up and walked towards my shirt , scooped it up , and walked away putting it on . I wanted to be left alone . I was sick of the control . I've been told what to do for 28 weeks now . " Fucking cunt loading my bergen " . I wanted for this experience to be over and start battalion life . And do some real soldiering . And make a name for myself . A lot of the guys came up to me . ' You're fucking mad! ' . At that point I thought 2 things . Why the fuck am I doing this out here . Everything . What am I doing here . And secondly , I've got nowhere else to go , I've got nothing else to do . Roy came to see me after and to be honest I didn't want to see him . I got a bit teary eyed

and upset and he was comforting and apologetic . I liked
Roy . He had a good sense of humour . He was loud and
outgoing . We gelled the rest of the week . He explained
that no one else would of done that but me . He told me
that a lot of these young kids want to be you . He gave me a
hug . A manly one . I wasn't responding . And he got the
message that I just wanted to be left alone . And so he did .
The rest of the week the platoon did more complex ranges
in Warcop . We did 1 man ranges where the targets pop up
and fall when hit . I enjoyed the rest of that live firing week
immensely .

We arrived back into camp from exercise and were told to
stay gated , so we could do admin from final ex , and then
prepare for the week ahead . Pass out week . I fucked it off ,
and went to Newcastle with Neill , who was back squadded
for a little misdemeanor of his own . And spent £550 in a
strip joint . It was a well earnt weekend and of course when
I came back . I was in the shit again . There was a burning
desire for about 3 or 4 days after that weekend to go to war
with Roy . Landing hurtful shots to his head , and put him
under life and death pressure . Andytown style . It took a
couple of days to replenish my body to a fighting state , and
his little ground and pound had slightly disjointed my
shoulder . I rang Victor and told him what happened and
what my intentions were . He calmed me down

' Mc Goo, Listen you're at the finish line , How long have
you been there '

' 28 weeks '

' 28 weeks for nothing , You decide , They'll fuck you out! '

I weighed it up . It left a bad taste in my mouth . But 1 more week to push .

Word had spread like wildfire about the incident with Roy and I , and then fucking off a direct order to stay gated for admin . To put it mildly , The Garrison Sergeant Major was not that happy with me and let me feel it every step of the way during pass out week . He was constantly on my back and gripping me . There was even talk of back squadding me again , which Mitchell was all for . I took a lot of shit of that 4ft nothing little squirt . The Garrison Sergeant Major . And he had me on pins and needles right till the end . He even decided to ring the battalion and give me a less than nice word . My name was in the shit before I ever rocked up . Thanks Sir! .

BATTALION LIFE

We went straight to battalion . It was a ghost town . The whole battalion was in Iraq on Telic 10 . Our pass out leave was taken off us because there was a distinct possibility that we were gona get the last month in Iraq , Telic 10 . I was looking forward to it . Contacts , doing attacks on buildings a bit of unarmed , or , armed combat with Al Queda , my imagination was running wild . We got there , filled sandbags for 30 days , then came home .

When we got back it was freezing , I'd only been there for a month . Had become climatised the best way the army knows how , beasting you physically and working you like a bitch . And then by the time I came home I had to start re-acclimatising again , which took longer . The cold really cut your throat and chest and arms , all over . Basically we'd did enough to get a medal (28 days) . Over there I tried to jump on as many patrols as humanly possible . I did about 12 in the warrior Armoured Vechile - Tank , and sitting in the back of it for long patrols killed your arse . I'm thankful to my full bloke Phil , Cheers phil .

You heard guys bitching about what we had done to deserve our medals , and being a bit anti-whoever just did a month . It was a bit unnecessary . It was like a holiday for me . The camp had a punch bag and I smashed my pft time. 8.05 . I quickly realised that not all G-men were equal . It

153

was weird . There was rank between the G-men (Guardsmen) . You have your junior G-men and then you have your Senior G-men , and the Senior G-men talk to the junior G-men like shit , and they don't even have any rank . I was a bit taken back at these kids talking to be like I'm beneath them in some way . I wanted to slap a lot of them , but I just sat back and observed did what I needed to do to the best of my ability , acted professionally and always keen , because I was .

When we got back to the UK . I quickly learnt that the rest of the battalion called 1 company CROW company , because that's where all the crows go . Straight from training . It's a young company and in many ways we were treated and talked to like we were incompetent , and many exercises and scenarios are set up to validate that . I really don't understand that way of thinking , and so rebelled , naturally . Some of the more senior companies would caw like a crow as you marched past , which would bring laughter from everybody , even the crows . I learnt what a red arse , or , a red bum is . If you're straight out of training you're a red ass , which means you're junior . Some of the senior blokes would call you a red ass with such venom , spite and authority . I never really understood it , but there you go .

You know I have a complex about being seen in a certain light , respected , appreciated , accepted , strong and resilient . Of which I know I am , or I believe I am . Being cawed out like a crow or called a red arse , would not feed this complex I have of myself , so when confronted with this , my swagger and resilience would come out . To the disappointment of nearly every senior bloke . Initially of course , but in time that would change . So we were based in Aldershot , and within a couple of days I targeted 2 or 3 people that were gona be a problem for me . They all seemed to be from up North and very , very mouthy .

1 was Dean he was a Lcpl . I distinctly remember him kicking a cigarette butt in my direction as he told me to pick it up . I turned away , ' *Nah your alrite I'll pick something else up* ' , as I went over to pick up a bottle . We were doing areas , picking up litter from around the camp , it's what we do every morning , before role call . I know for a fact that in the street back in Andytown this kid would not of even said Boo to a ghost , and now he's telling me what to do and not being too polite about it either . He was always saying deeply negative things towards me , ' *You're not a special snowflake Mc Gowan!* ' . The feeling in my head was – " Well I don't want to be a special snowflake . I'd like to be treated with respect " . ' *I have rations that've been in the army longer than you!* ' . So the rations in your webbing are more important than me . Cheers ! . It wasn't a nice welcome to Battalion .

2 was McGreary a Lsgt who threatened to throw me out a window when we were upstairs in the office " Fucking try it ya cunt " . He hated me and I walked away thinking " How dare you " . It was as bad as someone saying they were gona stab me . I wanted to get him alone and punch the fuck out of him . Show him who the real boss was .

3 was Einstein . He got this nickname because he was anything but . Einstein was built like Arnie , big and muscley

. But a big bitch , I knew he'd never been in a dog fight in his life . He was controlling and a big bully , especially to the younger more genetically smaller guy's in the company , and on a couple of occasions he'd pick them up and throw them if their rooms weren't presented correctly during room inspections . What kind of asshole picks up and throws some kid half his size . He picked his prey wisely . For about a year with me he postured , posed and threatened . Until I woke up one day and said ' this faggot ain't gonna do shit ' . It's all bravado . This posturing and threatening and lip is a big trick that only bullies use . His trick was not going to work on me , and never did . He stuck his hands on me one time , and I grabbed him back . MY heart was saying , " Fucking GO , GO , GO , GO " . I wanted him to hit me so I could put him in his place . He let go of me quickly and rushed into the office to get a show parade .

That was his party trick , writing me Agai's . A show parade is a punishment you get for a misdemeanor . It takes away your night as you have to show at 10pm and you get inspected . If you get bagged on the inspection the show continues to the next night , and so on . It seemed like I was on show parade the first year and a half of my battalion life . Solid . But it was fine they were going to break before me . What were they going to do give me push ups . I could bang them out all day and how can I say this with a bit of humility . I was probably the fittest bloke in Battalion those first 2 years . Definitely top 3 . I don't know what rank Einstein was , he wore a Lcpl rank slide . But he hadn't done the courses , and it showed . I didn't rate him as a man , a soldier , anything . He was a big fake in my eyes and when he found out the dates we were deploying to Afghan he ran to the office , and signed off . When you sign off you have a year left in Battalion before you go , and Deployment on Operations is not allowed .

He signed off to be a fitness instructor for a Health Spa . Plenty of action there . Tough guy . On reflection he was probably suffering from a bit of PTSD . He'd done Iraq . Still , his behaviour was inexcusable and disgraceful . He's the last person I would want by my side when it was hot and heavy .These 3 , Dean , McGreary and especially Einstein handed me out show parades like they were handing out candy .

If you were from Northern Ireland , these 3 would put you on barrack guard on the weekends , and let their own go home because they're all SAffA's . SAFFA is an organisation that exists within the Army , for people with family concerns . It's used in a derogatory way in battalion for the boys who go home to see their parents every weekend or get homesick i.e ' You're a SAFFA case ' . Because Northern Irish won't go home as often as the SAFFA cases from up North , because it's a commercial flight and more expensive , opposed to 200-300 miles in a car North . We were banged on more guards . It was unfair on the Northern Irish at times , but hey-ho , what's a barrack guard .

The reason earth can exist at all is because of the massive gravitational pull from Jupiter . It's like our solar systems Dyson , it has such a gravitational pull that it has 3 moons orbiting it , and it pulls debris and asteroids towards it and away from the earth . And these first 2 years , I had a similar role in battalion to Jupiter , these 3 saved so much debris for me that it meant many of the other new guys got through it unscathed . I'm by no way a victim , but when in a system that it's easier for everyone to be the same , or similar , I was undoubtedly viewed as an anomaly .

After about 2 years in Battalion they started accepting me as who I was . I guess people meet the truth with huge resistance before finally accepting that I am the way I am , and always will be . What also helped is my Quarter master Sergeant from my company and I became very good friends . He was studying Philosophy and just recently finished an open university degree that has took him 10 years . He's going for his Masters next . He's a very very clever man . His name is Bob and he's an absolute legend . Bob took one in the shoulder in Iraq in Telic 1 . He was just a stand up guy with no bravado and a great sense of humour . Well when we got talking we quickly realised that we had a lot in common , and we recommended and actually bought each other books that had impacted our lives . He was a higher rank than the trio and just through association helped me tremendously . If it wasn't for him the bullshit would have been going on much longer than it did . It all slowed down the debris flying my way . Thanks Bob .

You learn from the people around you . The first 2 years I carried myself somewhat the same way I did back in Andytown . I was defensive and didn't let anyone in , but I was impressed by a couple of people . Extremely very physically capable guys , but , and it's a big but , were humble with it and great with the boys . Great leaders of men . Great people persons . I took a bit from them . Up until then I proved what I could do physically . It was now 2 years in battalion that I decided to show what sort of human being I could be . This machine gives you a stage . A stage to perform all your best attributes , social , physical , moral . In and around this time I started trusting certain people . Bob was one . He nick named me Bonkers Bobby Mc Goo . He really settled me down and made me take a few extra breaths each minute , so to speak . Bob was great company and his presence had a calming influence on me . He was a very funny man . For a while I worked with him in the stores and he was great company , and I'm not ashamed to say that for the duration of my time working with Bob in the stores , I was his brew bitch . He really helped my transition into Battalion life .

Most of the people I came to trust were of a higher rank and there was a working class element to all of them . With me they didn't take the rank too seriously , they were all so proficient , and chose not to throw their rank down ones throat , whilst maintaining that human side to themselves . Bob's a real soldier , he uses his rank to develop the guys , not to oppress them . In an Infantry unit like the Irish Guards you're more or less married to it . The Battalion , the boys come first . Everything else , second . How families can stay together in the Army in the long run loses me . These families must have a unique and special bond . The rewards are great , guaranteed wage last working day every month means you can save , plan , buy clothes , have a car , insure it , it gives you stability . But ultimately it's very structured , very disciplined , and controls you massively . Monday to Friday , and it's not unheard of to be prepping your kit on Sunday night , for the week ahead .

In Battalion you're under one big microscope . Your character is put on display through physical challenges , Team work Exercises and day to day Duties . Where training is fast paced and physically intense Battalion is , like I said before , more structured , more disciplined . The job is so physical , so relentless and demanding , that the best way to do business is with pure heart . Attitude and ego don't last the long run . I believe that every soldier wants to go to war , just like every great athlete wants to win gold in the Olympics . Put will , skill and training to the test , while making a difference . And we do make a difference while we're there , but it can be unsustainable long term , unless certain systems are put in place for our withdrawal . Not forgetting the financial implications also .

I got a little bit of jip because I came from Andytown , from a couple of people from the other side of the fence . 3 in particular . It was all in good humour . The first 2 were from Potsy and Bryan P who were both from the other side . Potsy is from the Shankill and Bryan P is from Rathcoole . The first 8 weeks back from Iraq we were on a CFT . I usually sat at the rear . It wasn't important for me to be at the front . If people would struggle they would go to the front and I didn't fall into that category , so Potsy and Bryan P are behind me while I'm at the rear and I'm getting a couple of , ' *Andystowns!!!* ' and ' *Ya fenian!!!* ' from Bryan P in a slang Northern Irish accent thrown my way . When we get a ' PREPARE TO DOUBLE!! ' in training this was music to my ears , this little word of command . I chuckle and snigger at them before doubling . The double lasts a couple of hundred meters and I push it hard to try and outrun them . ' *What! ….Where the fuck do you think you're goin'* ' outbursts Potsy . I Leave them in my tracks but Potsy and Bryan P are very fit blokes in their own right and when they catch up with me that little bit of nonsense is over , and over the next year to year and a half in Battalion we become good friends . All for one and one for all .

Potsy'd wrap my door some nights at the weekend and we'd have a little boxing match in my one man room . Talk about a phone booth . He'd of been drinking so I'd slow the pace down and stay in the pocket and trade shots . I could of boxed the ears of him but I wanted him to walk away happy as well . As soon as we drew enough blood from each other and enough meaty shots had went in we'd touch gloves and put them away till next time . Usually the following weekend . A lot of drinking goes on in Battalion and the army in general . It's a drinking culture . I kept myself in good nick . I Would run at the weekends at night . Have the occasional bet to keep me distracted , but if I felt I deserved it and had worked extra hard in battalion I'd pick myself up a case of Guinness . The other bloke who gave me jip was big Cecil . A big country boy from Newry who looked like he'd be at home pulling potatoes and veg out of the earth with his bare hands . At first I thought his diction wasn't too good . He only knew 2 words ' *Alright* ' and ' *Provo* ' . Always the same two words in that succession . He'd always be passing me on his way to somewhere in Battalion , and without fail he'd query me ,' *Alright Provo* ' , it was a cheeky little tone . He'd say it in a perked up and surprised quip . I didn't react . Not for at least a year and a half and then when I was walking past him one day hurriedly on my way to somewhere in Battalion I queried him ,' *Alright Paisley* ' in a cocky tone . And eventually after about 2 or 3 years in Battalion we ended up having a conversation and he had a whole array of words other than ' Alright Provo ' . It was a long ice breaker but the conversation fermented wonderfully . He was rooted to his place of birth and very much brought that into Battalion , as did I .

Aldershot is a small Garrison town , it's basically a squaddie town . The boys go out in their masses every weekend to Yates or Vox . There are a couple of prolific shaggers in Battalion . If you are ever in a bar , and say that you're in the Irish Guards , and a woman mentions 2 or 3 names in particular , then you know to stay away as these women have already been ' Micked ' , which means a Mick Guard – Irish Guard has been there before . This never really applied to me as I always kept myself in tip top shape , and didn't go with the swarm to the bars on payday .

One night I even tabbed to Reading by myself , which is 20 miles away and a very lonely but enjoyable experience , it took me 7 hours , because when traffic came I had to stop , jump of the narrow country lanes on to the bank , and then continue . When I hit the 13/14 mile point I said to myself ' What the fuck are you doing out here , you fucking nutcase ' , I was in the middle of nowhere on a country lane , pitch black and the moon shining down . I took a gulp of water at this point and cracked on . When I rocked up at Reading I stopped at McDonalds and stuck something back inside me , maybe even a brew , and then I walked to the train station to get the train home . My intention was to tab the whole way back again . To Aldershot . From Reading . But for 7 or 8 miles of it I was running on the hard shoulder of a motorway/dual carridgeway and my feet were in a bit of a mess , even though I had a spare change of clothes in my daysack . I got the idea because I heard that Gordon Ramsey was a double marathon runner , I thought , I'll have a bit of that .

At times at the weekend in camp there'd be 8 rooms in our corridor and every door would be open . There'd be a party in every room and women walking from room to room . This all stopped , women , squaddies , alcohol involved . Women can cry rape and nobody wants that . So stricter rules were put on the gate that women needed to be signed in and were to be out at 11 . Forget getting a night's sleep when all that noise is going on around you .

Half way through my time in Aldershot the cookhouse was free , free scoff , they'd take £3 a day out of your wage before you even seen it ; and then they stopped it and introduced pay as you dine . When it was free scoff we were spoilt , absolutely spoilt : the food was great quality , and plentiful . When pay as you dine came in , they left the £3 a day in your wage but you had to vend for yourself , and every time you visited the cookhouse you had to delve into your own pocket . No dramas there , our corridors in the lines had little utility rooms with a washing machine , dryer and a little area to hang your wet clothes to dry , a fridge , kettle and a couple of hobs you could use to cook . I went to Tesco picked up some pots and food and squared myself away , as well as anyone who was in the lines when I was cooking . But this intervention with the pay as you dine threw a lot of the boys off kilter . On pay day some of the boys go on the piss from Friday right through to Sunday and spunk a lot of their wage , sometimes up to £500-£800 on alcohol and God knows what else . They might only be getting paid double that , so half of its away in the first weekend so they rely on the cookhouse for sustenance . You take that away , a lot of the guys had a hard time budgeting for this new unexpected cost of food . Instead of the boys going hungry , they introduced a ' hungry soldier scheme ' . It's like a ticket you get from battalion HQ , a dinner ticket that lasts you the rest of the month . You go to the cookhouse , show your ' hungry soldier ' dinner ticket to the chef , and you eat till the ticket runs out , usually payday . The ticket represents a lot of things . It's like a letter from your parents showing that you can't look after yourself and that you're incompetent . When Jarvis came to battalion he went to 4 company , I went to 1 . I called in to his lines one day and he had a hungry soldier ticket . I was taking the piss out of him , he was just back from skiing in Switzerland with the Army after 3 months . His response to me was , *' I'm a hungry hungry soldier Sergeant '* in a derisory brummie accent , and we'd both burst out laughing .

Were as before , the boys ate what they wanted and how much they wanted . Even if the chef said , ' Take *one* sirloin ' . If I had just came back from something and my body was depleted . I took what I needed . If I needed 3 sirloins , I'd look at the chef square in the eye and let him know just by my look , " I'm taking these 3 sirloins , these 3 sirloins are mine " and then I'd lift them . The chefs didn't look like they went hungry , and after a beasting if its free dining then I'd put back into my body what the program was taking out of me . And it wasn't always steaks , an extra fillet of chicken or fish . If I felt I needed it , it was on my plate .

What the job takes out of you is a result of some crazy physical shit , even by my standards . When in 1 Coy 12 mile log races round the area with kit on and weapon in hand , it transcends physical fitness . A log race , a massive log with handles on it , it's not about physical fitness but mental strength . These exercises condition and test a person's mental strength . With the Bravo Two Zero saga , Chris Ryan tabbed 400k in a couple of days with minimum water and food to the Syrian border . He lost every toe nail in the process . Such trauma and pressure on the feet causes this . On a course I lost my 2 big toe nails myself , in Belfast I would run 100-110 miles a week sometimes but then I was on my own time , in my own schedule , not being beasted by some DS , and never did I have a hint of losing a toenail . When it happened to me it was very painful at first , and a little shocking . I was very attached to my toenails . Certain areas of my feet I developed hot spots , that's were certain spots of your sole have become tender and painful to touch or put pressure on . They usually hit the nerve , and are always in the exact spot needed to run effectively (which is why they become hot spots to begin with) . I prefer blood blisters to hot spots . They again happen under the hard skin of your feet and are soft areas filled with blood and fluid , but you can start the recovery process by puncturing the blister with a sowing needle and letting the blood and fluid escape . When the blood and fluid escapes and the skin dries out it's all good . Once the skin on the balls of my feet broke off completely . The whole surface area . It was 3-4mm thick , and dead , and just fell away from my feet like a piece of plaster board hanging from a ceiling . In the Infantry management of ones feet is a prime factor to being able to soldier . Feet are basics .

Einstein

Doing the same thing over and over again and expecting different results

Einstein was a big strong boy with muscles bulging from every orifice . A vain body beautiful type who was sickeningly arrogant . Without fail he talked to you in an aggressive and angry tone and tried to be intimidating in every way possible . It was exhausting for him and everybody around him . He even spat on the ground aggressively – Ohh . Very . Very . Scary! . I found his intimidation tactics primitive at best . I'd seen it all before . He was constantly setting up things . Scenarios , incidents , trying to get me to react , to things , or not at all , which would evoke him to take actions on my insubordination . To be honest a lot of the time he simply lied to achieve his goal . I let it run its course . It did feel like a Patient / Therapist relationship . I was the therapist and he simply acted out , playing out all his bullshit on me . He behaved like it was his birth right to do so , to treat me and anyone he pleased , like this . I was relatively new in battalion and he had rank . He said what he wanted and got his own way for about 2 years until my Csm and company commander realised ' Hey , hold on , this kids alright , maybe the problem is Einstein ' . 2 years . Every working day . I went with him , every step .

Anybody who stands in front of a company while the G-men are stood on parade either to attention or at ease (this is with their hands neatly behind their backs) holding a cup of tea or eating an apple like a prize . While the whole company are staring in his direction . This sounds silly to the civilian but when it's done in a superior like manner like , " Look how far I've come in this place where you have to stand to attention , you 50 blokes **, I've** stood you to attention , looking in on me , big important and all powering me , I can stand here displaying a cup of tea or an apple , you can't " . And you're basically stood to attention facing him and his direction while he's centre stage , eating up everyones glares as he makes his statement . He is centre stage with an audience of 50 strong who have been ordered to stand to attention looking at him eat his apple or drink his cup of tea like you don't even exist . Good for nothing but to participate as his personal audience . All the time feeding off the attention of the 50 men he has stood to attention to face him .

This is power in the wrong hands . He stuck so much energy into his " angry man act " it's not surprising he didn't have the energy for anything else . Say to actually do some real soldiering . He'd use his control to draw energy out of the people directly beneath him in the rank structure . Just messing them about and making them do useless tasks . These people were like his blood , and I point blankly refused to engage in this transferal of energy from myself to him as an authority figure . Even though I knew my position and stance weakened his position and his ego , especially in front of the rest of the company . I decided " fuck him he ain't no NCO " , in the same position I would not be treating my fellow man in this way .

This type of behaviour gets under ones skin , makes them resent the position they're in , the job , the unit , for allowing such nonsense to take place which in turn damages the effectiveness of the battle group . A happy soldier is a good soldier . I became what I did despite his behaviour , not because of it . I became a descent soldier . The in-camp stuff is all there to build and establish trust so that when you go away with the boys and you do the whole band of brothers thing together , they know you and you know them .

I was a marked man in battaliion because of my swagger and rejection of other peoples bullshit . I wanted to pursue my Army career with a sense of integrity and purpose . Undoubtedly that entails separating yourself from the pack , like I had done so many times before , and not getting swallowed up by the trivialness of the day to day squabble of battalion life . I was direct in my dealings with people . I was in the Irish Guards to do a job not to socialise . This was at first . When it came to physical fitness or runs I was always top3 comfortably . Like in Andytown I was willing to go to extreme lengths to get that respect , and did , everyday . An Infantry Unit can become a very Machiavellian and cut-throat environment . The environment is competitive and people won't always play by the rules . The lower ranked NCO's are supposed to act with honesty and integrity . It's very rare that they will be called into question by the hierarchy .

Einstein's thing was to make you feel the clear divide between his rank and yours every working day . Sometimes a show of character isn't just what you're willing to do but also what you're willing to never do , regardless of the circumstances . In saying this the majority of NCO's are real good blokes . The flip side to that is not too pleasant to look at or be around , as I've alluded to before . The rank transforms some personalities into big , bad , ego's with loads of attitude . The power hungry and obsessive personality type will cease to live outside the 4 walls of the barracks , because this level of power and control can never exist for them in the real world . They need the constraints of the Army to provide them with it . I will be honest , when it came to Einstein very real thoughts did go through my head of taking sever action into my own hands , action that would of shortened my army career and ultimately changed the direction of my life . But my life was more than lowering to some fools level and I decided that he knows not what he does , and internally I labelled him a silly boy .

When I first met him he was carrying a cruel and scornful look . This look was permanently etched all over his face , like the very sight of a soldier lower ranked than he brought him deep pain and discomfort . I would become very familiar with this look of his . At first it bothered me , that he was behaving like this and was not tasting something boney and lightning fast across his chin . I found this to be very rude . We weren't given any other outcome but to be around him . He was a higher rank and in the *same* company . The first thing he ever said to me was after 3 days in the company after returning from Iraq and everyone was back from their lengthy post deployment leave . We were outside the armoury , ' *Ha! You're the trainee Guardsman that got smashed in training* ' he stood superior and tall , sphinxlike with an expectation that him simply bluttering out some nonsense . I would be happy to jump into the small box , that on the spot , he had just designed for me .' Yeah that's me ! ' I approached him with a big grin on my face , and put out my hand countering his negative comment with a kill him with kindness demeanor . I put my hand out to shake his . My positive energy smothered his lowly negative vibe , ' Pleased to meet Ya! ' , I said enthusiastically . He looked disappointed . That's right Einstein . You're not going to put me in my place with words , and from that day on the fun began .

He went to deeper and deeper lengths to get under my skin and take control of my soul . Only he could never of imagined what lengths I was willing to go to hang on to it . Even within the constraints of the army and handling a narcissistic bully with a higher rank . I was here for the long run and it was a test to see who breaks first . I was willing to step into the pocket that he was creating for me and beat him at his own game . To step in to the pocket where he is throwing serious psychological abuse and drama my way , and while he is wrapped and twisted in his conviction to break me or alter my mindset towards him . I continue happy , unmoved and resolute in the direction my army career is going , even though the mountain of shit is growing by the hour in my company towards me , because I am new and will not be brainwashed . Under their repulsion I feel fear and it brings me strength .

At first no one in the company likes me except the people I know from my pass out platoon , 21 Platoon , who have joined the company with me , and even they hide their acceptance of my personality under such harsh , new antipathy . Rumours spread that when Einstein was a young Guardsman he was bullied . I couldn't of cared less . Who hasn't had their knocks . Wouldn't it of been more inspirational if he *was* , and decided not to do it on anyone else . Wouldn't *that* have shown real character . But he decided to go the other way and because he was bullied at the start of his military career he made , or tried to make everyone else suffer for what happened to him when he first joined . That was his only true main dedication . He carried the , ' well it happened to me when I first joined ' gene , which is a low level place to be .

In the same week as he attempted his first little power play . Referring to the incident in training with Roy . We were at the back of the company offices waiting for work duties and his game plan of complete control of me was becoming more frayed by the day , ' *You're just a junior Guardsman!!* ' , he declared spontaneously with real venom and spite , trying to put me in my place verbally once more in front of the rest of the company . I was brand new , absolutely not even days in my new company since I came back from my month in Iraq . Maybe this was his well devised plan . To take control when they're unawares , new , unsettled and uncomfortable in their new surroundings . Let them know who's boss from the beginning . Then he charged me like a bull to a matador . I poised , took a look at him , and shook my head , like I was let down by what was happening , and then walked away a few metres from him . It was then that he accused me of tutting . I don't think I've ever tutted in my life , and if I did it was pre primary school so long ago I can't remember . Some of the other NCO's butted in ' *Oh...*

Is he tutting now! ' . Something like a tut in my father's house wouldn't of went down too well , and it wasn't in my make up either . I didn't enjoy the complex he was trying desperately to put on me. I knew that this was going to be a long drawn out thing .

His desire to put me in my place and make me look beneath him would eventually expose him for being nothing more than a bully and reveal me for being a man of considerable character . But this intervention wasn't going to happen any time soon . It was gona happen much further down the line . It could be both great entertainment , and exhausting , for the rest of the company looking in . I imagine it was both at times . I was always stuck in his section in field exercises , where at night he'd constantly be getting lost , and forgetting where the harbour area was . ' It's over there ' , I'd point and show him and get a 3 hour stag on sentry duty instead of 2 hours for my efforts , for making him look foolish in front of the rest of the section .

Everything he said was aggressive . I never once heard him treat a lower rank than him with respect . After a couple of months in battalion we got called out of our rooms to the corridor and I had my top off , *' Fucking bunch of hard cunts here!! '* he said in a snidey tone . Referring to me with my top off . " Why d'you wana find out about it! " . Every time he opened his mouth to me it fueled me to want to hurt him . I did offer him out once . While I was standing to attention formed up in the morning he charged me and tried to intimidate me , *' What the fuck d'you say! '* of course it was in an aggressive tone . I hadn't even opened my mouth . I stared at him '

Nothing ' , I replied in a calm tone , my eyes were piercing into his . Not just into his eyes , into him . His eyes were blank and empty . Fruitless . So was his soul . But the front he stuck on was massive , enough to trick the untrained eye . Hostility were I'm from is as constant as the wet weather . ' *Nothing What??!!* ' aggressively . ' *Mate!!??* ' . ' Mate , Nah not mate ! ' in a '' you fucking kidding me '' tone of voice . I looked at him like I'll never be your mate you prick . What have you done to deserve a mate like me . With some of the younger boys this is their cue to put their tail between their legs and say , ' *Sergeant* ' , Well forget that Einstein I'm not your mate and you're not putting words into **my** mouth . He might of grabbed me , I can't remember but as he walked away I continued my conversation as I was formed up in the ranks . ' Yeah you're a big man with them 2 stripes on your chest ' , in an almost questionable tone , like you wouldn't be trying this , nor getting away with this if it weren't for these four walls . ' Aren't ya'? ' again goading him . Questioning his motive , his resolve . I gave him a look that suggested , '' your pathetic '' .

I walked past him on my way to the office for an Agai . I was instructed to go to the office by him or another NCO and so made my way to the front door of the building . As I put my hand on the front door handle I received an almighty push . It was Einstein . I was asked to go to the office and now he's preventing me , being physically forceful and pushing me from behind . This isn't soldiering or for the greater good of the Irish Guards . This is about personal gain . In that moment he'd crossed the line . I'd had enough . I quickly jumped over the rail separating the building block from the drill square , ' Lets go then! You wana go!! ' , my head was starting to pound with all his bullshit .

In Andytown his behaviour towards me would of equaled to at least 12 events of physical violence . My body and mind were at one with my surroundings . I'd made it alright with myself for this to happen now . I felt peace with myself . This was going to happen . My body was ready . Within 4 seconds he'd about turned , made his way upstairs , had his head out the office window and was shouting and instructing , ' *Get him fucking up here noo!* '. I went up . I'd had enough . The guardsman wasn't walking up them stairs towards Einstein the rough , tough kid from Andytown who had dealt with this nonsense before was . ' *If I say stand to attention!! . You stand to attention!!* ' he shouted in my direction . ' *If I leave my dirty boots outside your door! . They're clean the next day!* ' he stated . '' Fucking leave your dirty boots and you'll find out that's not true '' . He was running from room to room in the company offices like a headless chicken trying to gain strength from everybody else in the offices . And with his sporadic momentum he was shouting this and that . I was far from standing to attention . I was worked up with left foot forward in his direction , towards the direction he was throwing his hissy fit ready to release an onslaught . It settled . I was worked up and taken to a room to settle down . What followed was a couple of 3 month warning orders for me . Not good and very uncomfortable .

You basically can't make any mistakes for 3 months and your full bloke writes reports on you every day . He goes through your whole day from start to finish . Every day surgically with precise times of where you fucked up and when . I found the whole process very invasive . You're

174

stood there to attention like an ironing board while he sits relaxed in the hot seat and tells you how much of a naughty boy you've been . Then when his greatest attempts to treat you like you haven't even reached puberty yet , and that your existence is nothing but a minor inconvenience to him , something he does before he returns to his wife and kids at the end of the day . After all that you have to ask him for his leave to carry on . Then your dismissed , when he says so , and you repeat that process every day for 3 months . It's dogshit .

12oz gloves or SA80A2

If you're perceived not to be playing the game , and the game is whatever *They* say it is then *They* can make life very difficult for you indeed . I've never been one to fall into line and so my initial time in battalion can be described as difficult , especially for the rest of the company trying to handle *This problem* . What's so hard to understand ? . I wanted to remain myself . The person I had groomed , carved and conditioned myself to be . The bravest of a pack , any pack . A hard worker . Someone who knew his true value , and was prepared to go through anything to let the people around him understand it . I wasn't going to present myself a certain way and then when Afghan came up , cower away . If death was my ending result of my stance . Then so be it . It was done my way . I didn't need the battalion for validation for some sort of identity . I was enlightened by this stage of my life to who I truly was . I was a warrior and would of found my feet eventually within the company and battalion as a whole . The aggro , the nonsense delayed that . Which was probably the whole point of it . Relationships had been forged over many years by existing members of the battalion , and I waltz in , this upstart , with a " I'm here to help but don't give me any aggro attitude " .

Yeah I had absolutely nothing my own way for the first 2 years , but so did probably every other soldier who started as a G-man . Unless they came in off the back of an uncle , or cousin , or brother . Someone like this they're path would have been much smoother , but then someone like this would of played the game . Knew what they were getting themselves in for . Knew how to play the game and more importantly , would of wanted to play the game . When they handed me a pair of drill boots in training I thought the drill was optional . Like there was a way to get round not doing drill , there wasn't , if you're told to march , you march , and if you don't you face the consequences and the consequences are not good .

The boxing team was off limits . When you're being made feel like you can't even iron your clothes properly and getting Agai'ed for absolutely silly stuff like boots not shinny enough or clothes incorrectly ironed , *They* put you in a state where you're always reacting . My body would react but my mind wouldn't , it was still and steely . Were if you're sensitive or open to it , it can damage ones confidence , ruin they're drive or even institutionalise a man . And this is where I came into conflict . The whole company knew about me . People talk . They write reports . Einstein tried to make his career with me . I was the Golden Cow . The one to be conquered . The one that didn't buy into his bullshit . I let him and everyone watching know it .

The one who knew better . You try pulling your feet in to the Csm and telling him you wana box for the army when you're fighting a mountain of shit like that everyday your head raises of the pillow . I resound to the fact that I would never be in the army boxing team . If I can't do it my way then I'm gona face the music here , soak it up and show them what this Belfast boy from the heart of Andytown is all about . If you won't give me a smooth path to the army boxing team then I'm gona leave it that every man in this battalion is undeniable about how good a soldier I am . I will etch my qaulities into the mind of every fellow man in battalion through relentless hard work and dedication , and when the time comes . When the rounds are coming down the range in the heart of Afghan , you'll see what this upstart is prepared to do . This upstart from Andytown .

Einstein wanted me to hit him and openly bragged that it was his mission to get me kicked out of the Battalion and the whole of the army in general . The only time I would of intentionally let my hands go is if it was in a designated area and we were alone and nobody could break it up . Like mad max , 2 men enter and one man leave . But of course this was never going to happen . *I knew , just knew* that whenever he was not in that uniform and in civvie street he was as quiet as a mouse , he just had that look all over him , easy to play the tough guy and be superior when you hide behind your rank and you never leave your comfort zone . He'd of got destroyed if he tried the shit he got away with in battalion with any normal standing civilian with a bit of balls . Any civilian with a bit of something about him . He's one of the worst people I've ever met in my life , and I've been round some shit bags . A self confessed bully ,he once said ' I'm just naturally aggressive ' . That's one way of alleviating responsibility for your actions . It's genetic . Of course . There was nothing natural about him and I suspected the " anger " may of even come from steroids . He would smugly walk around with a false sense of accomplishment like his very existence was something that had never been witnessed before . In reality he was just like one of the aggressive bullying twats I would fight on the road in Andytown . Only the guys in Andytown actually had a bit of menace about them . They weren't just front .

Every Friday before you get knocked off at the weekend , the whole Battalion do a Battalion CFT . A CFT is a Combat Fitness Test . It's an 8 mile loaded march with weapon and 56lb's on your back . You march in ranks of three and the objective is to do 8 15 minute miles , which means you come in on the 2 hours mark . We march . We double . We march . We double . Double is run . A lot of the times we come well under 2 hours . When you march in your ranks of three you march penned in . There could be up to 20 rows of 3 , each row of 3 marches behind each other . 20 rows of 3 equals 60 , which is about company strength . The NCO's float about either side of the main pack , usually on the right hand side of the marching group . As we were marching I was right hand side of the rank of three . When you march in ranks of three you're trapped within your little trio , by the guy in front of you , and you can't slow down because of the guys pushing the pace from just behind you . You essentially march as one impenetrable unit . As I was on the outside of my trio , Einstein came from behind from where I was marching . My right arm was my outside arm and I think I had my weapon locked in my webbing . My right arm was being used to power me forward . He quite purposefully and blatantly continually knocked my right tricep aggressively and with force with his forearm 3 to 4 times , enough to knock my right arm unnaturally high before stepping on into my peripheral vision , as if nothing happened , and to me it didn't . It wasn't the street and I had a bergen on my back marching with the whole battalion . My focus was on completion of the CFT , but it shows you the low level thinking of the individual to take the time to do such a thing . What did you think I was gona do Einstein , drop my bergen and attack you , that would be useless , wouldn't it Einsten . It would only make me look like a prat and I'd be biting the bait that you set for me .

I could understand this behaviour if he was an elite soldier , but at the end of the day he was just a jumped up Guardsman getting paid a couple of hundred quid more than me every month , and if you're behaving towards me in a manner that offends me , a manner that I despise then you're not gona get my respect , no matter what silly games you play . The way I felt about this guy , I wouldn't of sat in the same room as him in the real world . He had no redeeming qualities . Not someone you could say ' Oh he's difficult to work with but he's good at his job ' . He was useless , and used his overtly aggressive demeanor to disguise what was underneath , which was nothing . To be a good soldier you first have to be a good man . Soldiering is in your heart , it's something deep inside , it's the human spirit , it's drive , determination , it's noble and the job is difficult because it's so time consuming , it takes dedication , sacrifice . If you have a family there's a lot of time spent

179

away from them and a lot of training and field exercises .
Do you think for one minute I would of treated some kid
harshly or any differently just because he came to battalion
2 years after me , because I was more " Senior " than him .
I wouldn't , and I didn't .

TROOPING THE COLOUR MARCHING WITH PRIDE

Trooping the Colour was an emotional experience . We rehearsed that bad boy 70 to 80 times before doing it on the day in front of the Queen . At the end of all them rehearsals it was physically impossible to get it wrong . For 6 solid weeks Monday to Friday we rehearsed it sometimes 3 times a day . I was front row bang in the middle , Escort for the Colour . I never in my wildest dreams imagined that I would one day be giving an eyes right to the Queen . I never even knew what the Troop was . It's not something we watched in the heart of Andytown , but after seeing how much effort goes into a Trooping of the Colour and being part of the 2009 one . It was an honour to be part of such a special event . It's hard hard work and I might be guilty of being a bit biased when I say that the 2009 one was the greatest ever . It's the only one I have ever done and sadly will ever do . I do find it hard to watch at times , as I can clearly see Gdsm Chris Davies . He was the first fatality in Afghanistan in Herrick 13 when his callsign got caught up in an ambush , 5 were injured and Christopher was sadly killed . He was quirky and unassuming and our prayers are with him and his family always . God hold and protect you Christopher , Always .

When we arrived at Pirbright for our ' Spring Drills ' . That's what this 6 week of Troop practicing is known as . There was invariably loads of bitching and moaning from the boys

. ' *Should of joined the Para's , Less Drill , More soldiering , No Troop!!* ' . Boys a little late for the *should've's* when you're drill kits on , your bear skins on your head , your weapons in your shoulder and you're about to step off . Some of the Section Commanders were feeling the same as the rest of the boys , ' *Boys it's a shit sandwich , But everybody's gotta eat it , Lets get through it* ' . And that's all you can do. Nobody I've ever met could possibly enjoy rehearsing drill , The Troop , for 3 times a day for a solid month and a half but Infantry style you shut up , knuckle down and get on with it .

It's a great feeling after all that practice when you finally nail it . 50 Strong , Proud and Focused Men marching in unison and driving Forward at the same time . Everyone's feet are hitting the ground simultaneously wearing the Red Tunic with great pride in front of the Queen . It really is Magical and pure theatre at its best . As I was front row to the Escort and in front of the Battalion for those 6 solid weeks and on the main parade itself it showed me to be a hard worker and precise driller , and soon after that I was asked to jump on a RECCE cardre . That's Reconnaissance . No drama's to a bit of soldiering after all that drill , it's just what the doctor asked for . I loved the REECE cardre . It was awesome to be back in the field doing what I considered at this stage to be my real bread and butter .

RECCE TIME

I was attached to the Sniper Platoon for the RECCE cardre .
The Sniper commander I became very close to , throughout
my time in battalion . We talked boxing and life . His name
is Al and I attended the Sniper Platoon purely for him . I
valued my friendship with him that much . I knew my
shooting was good over 100 to 600m but I would
eventually find out that the L96 Sniper rifle is a completely
different weapon system all together and one that I
wouldn't get the time to master . The first or second day in
on the RECCE cardre the Sniper Platoon built a 6 man OP
(Observation Post/Point) it was started in the afternoon
and took 16 hours to build , all through the night under the
cover of darkness . We extracted about 8 tonnes of earth .
We laid our poncho's out flat like blankets and emptied the
earth onto them and dragged them away from the OP with
the earth and the soil on top of them so as to prevent
staining the grass that surrounded our OP . We ran out of
poncho's half way through our digging , so had to tip the
soil on the grass anyway . You could of filled the OP with
water and swam in it . It was massive and we had great
eyes on our objective , and for the next morning the 6 of us
from the Sniper Platoon were in , and in our routine . We
stayed in it for about 6 hours , filled it in and then moved to
our next lesson .

We were given another objective to observe and left to our

own devices . We had to observe a particular stretch of road . We found a big bush with good angles and arcs , so we crawled in and cut the insides of it out and lived in the bush for 3 days , all 6 of us . It took the DS's (Directing staff) 3 days to find us as we were that well hid . Even with an 8 fig grid reference the DS's couldn't find us , and we had to break cover and guide them in .

The other sections on the Recce/Sniper cardre weren't as switched on as the Sniper Platoon , and when the Recce commander who was running the course came round to check the other OP's he caught the guys napping . They were sitting there with half-finished OP's with their helmets off , tucking into their rations . He just walked right up on them , and after a couple of days when the OP's had been collapsed and everyone had been centralized he took his revenge on everyone . After a 2-3 minute tirade about people monging it , he sprung his surprise . A stretcher was introduced . A proper one . Your poncho can be used as a stretcher , as it can be folded in half lengthways and there's handles knitted into it . It's what we used the whole way through basic training , but not this one , this was a proper bad boy stretcher .

' Alright you fucking mongs , Fucking Casualty !! , Nick D , You're the Fucking Casualty !! , Get Down You've just been shot in the Leg – Now Fucking Deal With It . '

FFD and a tourniquet was quickly introduced and applied .

' OK Get This Man on the Stretcher – The HLS is 3 Miles That Way !! .'

I was reunited with my old section commander from 19 Platoon , Caff . We both knew the score . He was one of the DS's .

' Alright McGowan!! Get on This And Beast these Cunts ! Fucking Drive this Forward ! .'

Caff knew I had a sadistic pleasure to physical pain and pushing myself to physical exertion , emptying my reservoir and then going to places deep inside me . Tendons burning , hands swelling , heart pounding , mouth foaming , feet and knees burning . He'd witnessed it before . It was like my Kauto Star Cheltenham - Gold Cup moment . Heart and grit and focus and doing it with a willingness that would inspire the boys around me to dig deep and go to places they'd never been before . What I loved about Kauto Star isn't just that he was a born winner . As a horse he was so strong and relentless and he was an entertainer . When he jumped the fences he looked majestic and graceful , not like he was in the middle of a race at all . When it came to a Pft or a stretcher I would put my chest and chin high and poised to the horizon and go , just like Kauto Star .

Nick D Jumped on the stretcher and there wasn't a mark on him . He'd done the course a couple of years in a row and he had rank . He'd proven himself as a competent sniper on IraqTelic 10 . Nick was 16 stone of stocky , South African muscle . By the end of the casi-vac as we edged closer to the HLS . The stretcher was broken and Nick had been dropped that many times that he had a dislocated shoulder and his right eye was gushing blood , he still has that little battle wound today . It was hilarious . He had to jump on the stretcher and be casi-vacced before he sustained his injuries and if I wasn't foaming at the mouth driving the thing forward I'd of been laughing at Nick's face as he had a resounded look on his face as someone who was expecting to be dropped several more times . His face looked like a little owls with big white eyes and a little pouting beak waiting for the next drop . Awhh adorable . I said I'd be laughing but truth be told when I was in the field I was **always** all business .

3 miles of hard undulating ground through rolling countryside . Up and down with the stretcher with Nick on it like a heart monitor . Like I said , the stretcher was fucked . The handles came off which left it nearly impossible to hold for long periods of time with fattened , greasy palms . Your

grip being pulled and jerked by the other 3 men on each of the other corners , whilst everyone was driving in the one direction . Couple that with the weight of your webbing – strapped round your hips and your daysack with all your specialized kit , scoff , wet & warm kit on your back and your weapon system either strapped on your person or carefully carried with the free hand that isn't on the stretcher . That's the outside hand . Your helmet can end up every shape on top of your head . The physical effort creates stingy sweat which runs into your eyes . The sting comes from the salt that's deposited from inside your body onto your skin and then the sweat from your forehead brings it into your eyes . The stretcher is a very tricky assignment and sorts the men from the boys . You can be Superman but in the army it really counts for nothing unless you can work in a team . It took me 2 years in Battalion to realise this . Initially I still carried the *me against the world* mentality but as I became more and more accepted and less criticized and ridiculed for the way I was . I did wake up one day . A very clear shift had been made . It was in fact , after working so hard on the Troop , it clicked with me , " I really need to start working for these people now " . In other words I really need to start working **with** them . They were giving me a stage and a platform . Respect had been earned now and it's time to give it back . I can't let them down .

When I started the Recce cadre my legs and knees didn't feel like my own , and they don't till this day HaHa! I know -

bad joke . I'll move on . But we did that much drill that humping my bergen around felt a little alien . I became a little bit of a celebrity after the Troop . I did work hard and all the head sheds knew me . When on the Recce cadre the badge , Rsm , came into our harbour area with the CO (Commanding Officer) . He was asking for me . The badge is essential to the Trooping of the Colour : he orchestrates everything and personifies what drill is all about . He has to be the smartest man on the square and 10 times out of 10 he is . There was a couple of us tucking into stew .

Rsm ' So how you's gettin' it '

' Yeah alright sir , you know what we do here '

He was a sharp man he looked at me in the eyes waiting for an answer .

' We fill sandbags '

He was still looking

' You know what we do when we fill them …… We empty them '

His look was more intense . He was looking at me trying to work out if I was taking the piss or not . I was , but in a friendly manner . But before he could say anything I said :

' I watched the Troop on Tv . That was some sharp drill . You looked good Sir '

A compliment from a G-man to the Rsm about his personal drill was unheard of . As he walked away disbelieving what he'd just heard . I'd been in the field for 2 weeks , and that had just lifted my morale no end .

When on the cadre the word ' clip ' was used many times . When a soldier says that he's ' in clip ' , it means he's not in a good way . After a while in the field a lot of the boys will say ' my feet are in clip ' , for example . You can be in clip from sleep deprivation or working hard , and the longer you stay in the field and the harder the course is , the more in clip you become . Till some of the senior recce blokes started saying , ' I'm in Turbo clip ' . This was then shortened to 'turbo ' . After a while you can see the boys who are in turbo and all they need to say is ' turbo ' , about themselves or someone else to get a raucous laugh . The mind can become delirious , and some of the boys can look like they're moving in slow-motion after sustained lengthy exercises in the field . You inevitably can make little mistakes you wouldn't if you were getting a good nights kip , silly little mistakes that are pointed out by the DS's . You make mistakes , you get punished or talked to like a cunt . The British army demands perfection ; they have a moto of ' Train hard Fight easy ' and what they put you through on training exercises would rarely come to fruition real time , but you never know . The British army trains you for the worst enduring possibilities .

After completing the Recce cadre I had 2 choices . Join the Recce , or go for the Snipers . Recce was just plain old soldiering . Sniper's was much more difficult and challenging , and the Sniper Platoon seemed to be a lot more introverted , which suited my personality . The Recce Platoon were alot wilder and always out on the piss , more of an extroverted Platoon , that work hard and played harder . I went Snipers . It was a bad move professionally , as it had taken me 2 and 1/2 years to be a daddy on the SA80A2 with the help of Robbo from the Sniper Platoon , who gave me a couple of pearls . Cheers Robbo . You helped my shooting 10 fold . With an L96 Sniper Rifle , my shooting was piss poor . It didn't suit my personality anyway , being at the rear of the Patrol or in a sanger with a long-distance rifle . I prefer to get amongst it with the boys , and as close and as personal as you can get to the enemy .

After a year in the Sniper Platoon with support company , I would return back to 1 company . I enjoyed my time in the Sniper Platoon and became a better soldier . I soaked in the experience from the blokes around me and I enjoyed most working nights calling into the Sniper Platoon office to have lengthy or short , but meaningful chats with Al the commander of the Sniper Platoon . He was great company and great to work for . I was unhappy to go back to a Rifle company but I was treated kinder due to a change of NCO's , who were from my neck of the woods , Northern Ireland . They know who they were and it was nice to get a bit of home support . Cheers Ryan . Cheers Stevo .

But before my move back to 1 company and during the leave we all received after the completion of the RECCE cadre , I took a well-deserved holiday with my good friend Mo , his now wife Laura , OC and his partner Olivia . It was great to have friends in my life that were worthy and loyal people . Mo , Bob , Al . All these people I would have given my life for , as I would an Irish guardsman , but with these 3 I just mentioned it was an added bonus to have them directly in my life . All three were more senior than I , and from the get go of my army career in battalion they seen me for who I was and gave me instant validation . The only time a friendship like this had ever existed in my life before was in the Salvation army with Victor . All 4 of these people have what I can best describe as raw intelligence . To me this is the ability to live your life being true to the person you are with your ideals and vision of yourself , no matter how much shit your environment throws around you .

On the trip to Turkey I was the loose end , and when drunk and very animated on the plane over I met a lovely older woman . I was just so happy to get away and have the money for the first time in my life to go away with a group of people who I considered deep , dear friends . I got her number and had a mega time in Turkey , Marmaris . She went her separate way when we landed in Turkey but had already given me her phone number , and on the way home we were on the same flight and sat in exactly the same seats again , and the deal was done . 2 months later she fell pregnant . Her name is Helen and she's the mother to my big , beautiful boy , George .

I MEET HELEN

Helen is English and middle class and it would be fair to say that I was attracted to her because of this . She was different from the women that existed in my domain most of my life , her voice was fresh and invigorating not an ounce of slang . The west Belfast voice in a woman I can best describe as nails on a chalk board that is to me of course , only me . I like the southern Irish accent in a woman , it's soft and smooth .

What attracted me to Helen more than anything was that she had a motherly maternal side that I felt if I reproduce with this person my child will be safe , happy , well adjusted . More than anything this is what I seen and felt . If my child were to experience any of the things I experienced as a child then I will have failed as a man and a father , even though my childhood in Belfast made me a very hungry and determined person . That was never gona happen . I was never gona do that . What added to the attraction is that Helen is very well educated . She speaks a couple of languages and has a couple of degrees under her belt . Helen is a qualified and practicing therapist and understands enough about the human mind and human behaviour and everything that entails . It all impressed me . She had intelligence which is what I find most attractive in any human being .

As I was now in support company when I met Helen the control the army had on me slackened and I could now leave myself open to attracting someone like this into my life . Support company is a lot less controlled , you are expected to be all over it as you've served your apprenticeship in a rifle company . I would recommend that every soldier do 2 years in a rifle company , you don't get treated too well but you are a better soldier for it . After 2 years you know what the job is and your role . It's like that saying that just because you pass your driving test doesn't mean you're a complete driver . It may take another year or two to become the complete package , this is the same for soldiering and battalion . So I would do my 5 days , Monday to Friday , running , training , Exercises , Ranges , Ceremonials , and if I wasn't doing ceremonials on the weekend I knew I could go into London 30 miles from Windsor and cook , drink Rose , talk and have some release from battalion . It was a good ratio , 5 days in battalion beasting it out , staying strong with the boys , staying focused , sharp , trained and then Helen at the weekend .

A love for Golf Gti's I had as a child saw me buy a 3 series for £1000 . I had it insured third party and would drive in and out of London from Helen to battalion . It was my intention to get a motorbike when I had the time and money to sit my test , so I could nip through the London traffic a lot quicker to get to Helens . For 25 years I'd starved myself of affection from a woman . I was always pushing , striving , unhappy with my financial situation . A quarter of a century 23 of them in Belfast and 2 ½ in the army . Eventually I opened up and let Helen in , I was ready , the timing was right . I had money , enough money to buy

, insure and run a car . At this stage I was more of a senior guardsman so was earning more and not being pushed as hard as before . I was in many ways a complete soldier and could more than make things happen for myself and the boys around me . Helen knew a lot about foods and wine and Sky tv was quickly introduced to the home so I could watch the boxing at the weekend . She had a cook book and I would cook a different meal for us every weekend . Mainly fish dishes , as a child I never had many fish dishes , it was too expensive and I simply thought that the supermarkets never stocked it because my mother never cooked it .

I would charge my batteries with good food , good conversation and Helen and go into battalion for Monday morning knowing I had something to look forward to that weekend . We would go for long walks with the dog in Kent and stop off for a pint of Guinness , Helen would have cider . I loved the dog , I loved Helen , I loved that I was contributing to her life and she was contributing to mine . I loved that I was with this beautiful woman and she was not trying to change me , pressure me to be any different , she accepted me . It was a really special time in my life , I felt God was rewarding me and when Helen revealed to me that she was pregnant I knew it was going to be a healthy , strong boy . When the baby was conceived I was 25 , strong , healthy and at the peak of my powers .

DADDY GOES TO WAR BABY

When George was born it took all my worries away . I was a father , he was my son , and it was just a wonderful time in my life . It gets better and better every single day with that kid . It fell perfect and I ended up getting 3 weeks of paternity leave followed by 4 weeks of pre-deployment leave , all at the same time . It was 7 weeks of paid leave and the biggest chunk of leave I'd ever had in my 4 year army career . The house was full of love for little George . If I died in Afghan I was happy that I'd left my legacy , George , and Helen would collect £300,000 from my life insurance . In my head I was gona get wiped out , or come back with not a mark on me .

I thanked God for what he had giving me , a beautiful educated woman who loved me , who gave me a strong , robust , big , healthy boy . My life had more meaning than ever before , but there was a job to be done . I was gated at home with Helen and George for about 6 solid weeks . Helen had a c-section and needed time to recover . George was such a bruiser with a massive , big , perfectly round head when he came out , he looked like a pitbull . I couldn't believe that such a thing could grow to such a size inside the human body , he was massive with scrunched up features . An amazing experience , I thought '' Well if he's gona box or fight with features like that he's won the intimidation angle '' . Every 3 hours round the clock he wanted food , I was host , people coming round , champagne , wine , keeping the house , walking the dog , getting everything in from Tesco's . On one trip to Tesco I walked away from a fight , some black kid was throwing attitude my way ,

' You alrite fella you see something you like '

He came back at me ' Why you wana go brotha'! ' .

I walked away , I didn't have it in me , George's birth – round the clock love and care , Afghan in 2 weeks' time . The fight I was about to indulge in was a long , grueling 6/7 month fight with the Taliban . I couldn't pull myself back from my psychological process to engage in the confrontation . If it wasn't for George and Afghan it wouldn't of even got that far I'd of already been steady and would of simply pierced into his eyes without opening my mouth but I knew Afghan was looming close .

Just weeks away and a fight I had been pursuing since my first ice breaker with Davey Walker . Initially I said I wanted to check out Iraq and see what it was all about , because that's what flooded the media , but half way through training my friend Neill said ' Afghan , you want some serious war fighting , some serious soldiering , Afghan's the place to be ' , I never forgot it . We took a trip to the Cotswold's in the 6th week of my leave . My body and mood was starting to change . I was preparing to die or be killed . I wasn't a very good partner that week . I needed to be left alone to prepare myself for what was about to come and my role in it all . I left Helen's on the Friday and I didn't have to

be in till the Sunday . I didn't even say Goodbye . I just said '
I'm away ' , and left the house to jump on a train and start
the journey towards Afghanistan from Windsor . My mind
was already on the job . I was becoming cold and
emotionless and focused . I was preparing myself for death .

With a series of flights in a 20 hour period we made our
way to Bastion . When we arrived in Bastion we got our kit
and were allocated rooms . It was dark . The lights around
Bastion exposed a thick , dense dust which was spread
from the constant use of armored vehicles in the camp . It
got everywhere , nose , ears , eyes , mouth and all over
your clothes . We settled and prepared for the final week
before going on the ground . Brief's , fresh intel , objectives
, and zeroing weapons all took place in Bastion . As we
ripped in to begin Herrick 13 , the Jock Guards ripped out ,
and I bumped into Gibbo a section commander from 21
Platoon from training . He'd just come off the ground and
finished Herrick 12 . He looked tanned , sworthy , thin but
strong . He'd had a good tour . I knew just by looking at him
. He looked primed and in the moment , still ready for
action . We spoke for a couple of minutes . It was great to
see him . I'd mellowed over the 3 years from leaving depot
and it was great to talk , man to man respectfully .

We had heard bad news when the Jocks started Herrick 12 .
They weren't but a month in when Davey Walker suffered
Gsw . Gun shot wound . He was on a command task and
died of his injuries . From my friend Neill who was attached
to the Jocks at this time , he said that 1500 people turned
up at his funeral . It was a testament to the type of man he
was . He was a character with character and when his coffin

entered the church they played the Star Wars theme. He used to say that he was a Jedi and we were all his baby Jedi's . He can take credit in knowing that he was directly responsible for producing , shaping and molding over a thousand Guardsmen for their respected Regiments . A truly unforgettable character that must never be forgotten. For everything , Thanks Davey . The news of this was shocking to me . It emphasized the fact that no one was untouchable . CO's , Rsm's they were all getting killed . Such was the tenacity of the Taliban in Afghanistan . Where before you would hear of the occasional Private or Lcpl getting killed , no one was safe when they left that plane .

The FOB

After a week of OPTAG we arrived in our respected FOB (Forward Operating Base) . We were probably one of the most Northerly-located Bases . We dropped in at night with all our kit from a Chinook . We got a brew and got settled into our bed spaces . It was good to finally be there so we could count off the months and finally go home to a nicer bank balance . I got settled in and the next day sat on my bed and wrote a bluey (Military style letter) . It said something like " I've just settled in got dropped into the FOB last night from a Chinook . Could be another Iraq . Staging on and the occasional patrol . Think I'm pretty safe here " . Half an hour later all the boys were called to the briefing room to see the company commander . A small , thin man , very fit who earned massive respect from the boys for his honesty openness and genuine love for ' His boys ' .

It was my first time working under him as 1 company had been broke up and myself along with 10 others were attached to 2 company respectfully . He spoke with enthusiasm and ambition with a who dares wins attitude . I was listening to his plans . He was saying it like it was a scene from *Saving private Ryan* . Talking about going in under the cover of darkness and blowing bridges because it was a main Taliban supply route . Going into the heart of Pasab - the local Afghan village , using the element of surprise . Just being there and greeting them with a friendly Good morning as they woke up - catching them unawares . I went away feeling pumped and motivated I knew now that It was not going to be another Iraq and went back to my bed space and wrote another bluey to Helen , while the information was fresh . Both blueys were wrote within 45 minutes of each other and they were like chalk and cheese . I hadn't spoken to Helen for 10 days since arriving in Afghan and left it another 2 weeks before I picked up the phone . I was truly settled in my surroundings at that stage and could talk a lot freer . Over a series of weeks we engaged with the locals on a daily basis . The commanders got to know who the village elders and chiefs were and the intel building began .

The FOB is made of Hesco . A Hesco is a wire framed container with a camel coloured material that holds the sand in the wired frame . It's a 1m cube . These cubes are filled dense with sand and compacted down . These Hescos are built on top of each other like one big lego set . Rounds from small armed fire have been known to hit the body and not have left due to velocity . A bullet from a small armed weapon system won't travel through 1m of dense compacted sand . These were built 1 course thick and 3 high round the whole of the perimeter creating the FOB . It was like a big sand castle , our sand castle , our fortress where we ate and laid our heads at night . It was unlike the eye sore that loomed over Musgrave Park back in Belfast . A matt grey , corrugated iron , monstrosity . The FOB mixed in well with the surrounding landscape .

The FOB has 5 sangers all built of Hesco also , with good cam and good back drop , back drop is when you cam up the sanger so your silhouette and shape isn't easily identifiable to enemy or enemy snipers . Each sanger has interlocking arcs so the whole circumference of the FOB is covered . Inside each sanger there is a full range of equipment , these are some . A GPMG or a 50KAL or both , flares , a map of the ground in front of you with known points on the ground marked on the map , a radio , your personal weapon system always goes to the sanger with you . If there's any dramas you radio into control room on the radio . They're callsign is always '0' , and if there's anything suspicious you bring them on to it and tell them what you see . When you enter the sanger to start your stag you get a brief about what has just happened in the last 2 hours , if anything , by the guy your taking over from . He'll tell you if there's anything suspicious , anything you should watch out for , and then when you get relieved from your stag . You do the same for the guy taking over from you . This is called a sanger brief . You let them know if you've just changed the battery on the radio , or if they're stag falls in between meal time you can bring them up a plate , or relieve them for them few minutes so they can eat their scoff . They might need to take a shit , you can usually piss in a bottle , taking a shit in one - might not be the cleanest operation , and so someone is needed to cover for them while they do so . Passage of information is essential .

Patrolling the area – making observations

Before we go on patrols , especially major ones , we have a brief in the briefing room . There's a map the whole surface area of the table in the briefing room . The map is laminated . We gather round , one row sit , the other behind them kneel , and look in for instructions . The seats that surround the table are made of Hesco . The Hesco seats cover 3 sides of a square around the table . Whoever's giving the brief for my section takes centre stage , or stands and talks , while everyone else sits or kneels , that'll be Miller my full bloke , or J-Dog , my platoon commander , or AB . Everyone is vital to the team and given their own individual role within the section or the multiple . If it's a big OP they might go into finer detail on a white board that is on the wall . The white board is on a wall with no seats in front of it , so everyone round the table has a clear line of sight at it , and can look in . This is what happens in a brief , callsigns are told where they'll be and when , our main objective on the ground , we're told the stages of advance , the attack , SOP's when contacted , SOP's for casualty abstraction , possible HLS for that abstraction if a casualty takes place . Everybody has a job and everybody knows exactly what they're doing before they step out the gate . On the first patrol we were approached by a local teenager from the area and Chris Tobin made an observation , ' *D'you see the size of that cunts feet!'* , he said in a quirky and rather bemused Southern Irish accent .

It was a kid we would become very familiar with , as he was always all over our patrols , as soon as we left the gate . Locals coming close is always dangerous until trust is established , suicide bombers can be a threat , even when trust is established . But if that's the case 9 times out of 10 we usually have the heads up , we hear it through the locals , intel . We know the basic command words in their language if such a threat seems possible . Stop . Lift your dish dash . Turn around . Back to the kid with the big feet . Ok Chris , if you put a gun to my head and ask me I would probably say that this young man's feet are disproportionately big for a kid that age . But my immediate focus was on the job Christopher , the job . It wasn't the feet but his delivery of his question that brought a smile to my face . We're over getting a feel for the place and your laughing at some locals feet .

We quickly learned why their feet were like this . A lot of them had no footwear . Some of them wore crocs , or something similar . When flooding poppy fields the Afghanies have ingenious little ways of manipulating the rivers that surround their homes and fields . They build little barriers like beavers , stopping the flow of the river and directing it were they choose . The barriers create the flood and the fields are designed like a structured maze , filling up specific sections of the field bit by bit like a jig saw . The pieces of the jig saw are separated by little walls of top soil piled up , about a foot high . Well , kids like this one that approached our patrol . They create these little walls by driving a spade into hard stony soil . They do this bare footed , driving a steel spade with a bare foot into the ground will definitely change the shape of one's feet . And there's the answer . Chris Tobin is a great soldier , I was on the Recce cardre with him . The reason I believe he was so good , apart from his skills , ' Passage of Information ' , he loved talking , he could talk for Dublin . Chris is a stand-up guy with a good heart .

Leading from the front

For the first 2 months all we seemed to do was interact with the locals , build intel , and do the occasional purposeful patrol . We would push out as far as we can to see were our flet is . That's where we get contacted from . Our flet is the limit we can push to before being contacted , and what land we can safely patrol on , and dominate . The first time I was shot at it was exhilarating , the rounds came within a couple of metres of me . We advanced a click (1km) into deep territory . We cut through hedgerows with a pocket knife , went through rivers , and patrolled through large corn fields that were over 2m high . I was point man , as we pushed the flet , I told AB on the PRR , ' There's 3 times PAX here Sir ' . AB , ' Call them over ! ' . AB rushes to the front through the cleared lane to get closer to my location . He arrives . 20m behind me . I point . He calls them over . But they are looking at me and as we march they are 90m away , and at 9 o clock . I repeat the command because I am closer . The command sounds like ' Del-Da Rossa ' . It means ' Come here ' . The three teenagers scamper away quickly through a hedgerow and out of sight , and it's within the next 15 steps on my axis we get contacted from an AK47 , 70m away to my right flank at 2 o clock . The rounds crackle over the top of our heads as the bullets make mini sonic booms breaking the sound barrier . As they spear the ground they create rash and violent eruptions from the soil beneath our feet . It sounds like a cheap firework display going on all around us . A cheap firework display with potentially lethal circumstances . I empty half a mag in the general direction the AK47 is coming from before we extract . I am point man and it's then I decide I want to be point man from there on in . It's the most exciting and it's where the trouble usually comes from . I have a chance at being shot at first , see who and where they're doing it from , drop to a knee and do a bit of damage myself . Although we are susceptible from the attack to come at any angle .

However we are usually marching directly towards it . Being trained for the attack coming from any direction is what's called having three-hundred-and-sixty-degree awareness . The army trains you to have eyes on the back of your head and know what's going on all around you at all times , three-hundred-and-sixty-degrees .

When point man your weapon is strapped around your front . Because the equipment to detect high metal content from the ground . Is in hand . My case – right hand . As point man I can have my weapon strapped around my chest and within ¾ of a second I can have my weapon in my shoulder , be in a fire position , click the safety catch off , pumping rounds or UGL's at a target . Not just that . I wanted to be point man because I didn't want one of the junior G-men who'd just rocked up , not comfortable in the

Platoon and section not doing the drills correctly , and leading us into harms way . Subsequently I was the senior G-man to the new blokes that wasn't there for me when I first rocked up . It wasn't but 2 months in when we got our first real casualty . We were on a fighting patrol and we were taking on a compound named ' Crazy compound ' . A fighting patrol is when you leave the FOB and you're looking for a fight with the Taliban .

Gill becomes a casualty

While pushing out to see where our flet was we had continuously been contacted from this compound . It was named Crazy compound for the obvious reasons . We left the PB (Patrol Base) closest to it . I was in the Fire Support patrol to the side , while another callsign was patrolling more or less head on . From our PB ' crazy compound ' was 600m away . The fire support team I was in was gona locate around 300m away from Crazy compound , to give adequate fire support for the other section patrolling head on , if and when they needed it . 150m away from the PB and 450m from Crazy compound Gill was hit by an IED . I remember stepping off from the PB thinking it was a beautiful morning . It was very early , and the air was crisp and cool . The rising sun in the distance looked like a vanilla sky . It looked beautiful and picturesque . Like a Monet landscape .

5 minutes later we were casi-vaccing Gill with 2 legs missing right up to the knee . It was shocking . Initially I thought it was an IDF . InDirect Fire-Mortars . I shouted ' **Fuck their close!** ' . There was dust everywhere and nobody

knew what the fuck was going on for about 30 seconds . Initially the dust created a blanket that hid the chaos beneath it . I was the 5th man on the patrol , and Gill was the 7th . OC was between Myself and Gill , and was blew forward with the force of the blast . I said to OC , ' who was behind you '

OC , ' Gill ' , at that he shouted **' Gill!! '** .

Gill replied **, ' What ! '** in almost vexed tone . 2 of us thinking it couldn't be Gill . 5 seconds later the dust cleared . It was Gill and he was in a mess . I was as cool as a cucumber telling the point men to go back and clear up to him so as to start our abstraction . They did . Chris Tobin was first at hand , ' Gill are you alright mate ' he said in his soft southern Irish accent as he slowly removed his tourniquets and put them on carefully with what was left of Gill's legs . It was like a Great White had bit his feet off with his razor-sharp teeth . What was left of the bone was black and scorched and sharp . Imagine a kebab skewer and half of the meat missing . With the skewer acting as bone . It looked similar n ratio and in shape . The tips of some of his fingers came off as his gloves were gently removed . We were all working and worried for Gill .

Gill's breathing was constant and increased . More sudden . His belly swelled . His vital organs and lungs increased working . To subdue and control trauma that his engine had just suffered . The golden hour had just started and time was- a- ticking . Each minute felt thick with promise . Hope . Purpose . As if we were all digging into our own souls . Our own resources . Telepathically trying to give Gill all the strength he could need at this point in time . Hoping it would be enough . Until the medics who had seen this time and time again got their expert hands on him . Carin our medic done a wicked job . She quickly administered morphine . But on the field ones resources can be limited for an injury this traumatic . Tourniquets were on . Pain relief had been administered . It was now time for the abstraction back to the HLS which was in the PB we'd just left from . Get him on the chinook and off to Bastion .

Sweeny his full bloke was on the stretcher ' *You fucking hang on , you're a fucking legend* ' , he was panting , shook and emotional . We hit the PB . . His body looked soft and sensitive . Tender . He lay there in the PB . Reminded me of a baby who'd gorged too much milk . Belly swollen badly . Breathing fast and frantic . The slightest jerk and movement drew immense pain , which put the survival process in the balance . We secured the HLS , then seen Gill on and off to the chinook . When the Chinook took off and the dust settled we were all disheartened , and I don't know what anybody else thought but I thought that because of what happened to Gill the Op would have been cancelled . Oh was I wrong .

' Alright boys get your fucking kit on we're heading out again in figures 5 ' . No more beautiful Vanilla skies it was a fully-fledged morning . The sun was coming out and the heat was coming up .

We stepped off again on route to our fire support location . We treaded each step with extra vigilance passing were Gill had just been hit . There was no more dust but an errie silence loomed around the area where the IED had been detonated , and as we patrolled we passed the crater that had been left . Thick dark blobs of blood were on the ground with a coat of dust that speckled the blobs , and pieces of Gill's kit that had been blown off in the blast were now visible . We retrieved them as we passed stuffing them in our daysacks . Protective eyewear . His morphine kit . A magazine was now visible . We passed and continued on our mission . By now the Patrol advancing more or less head on to Crazy compound came under contact from small arms fire from inside and around Crazy . It was on . We moved methodically and carefully into position . We could hear a GPMG (General Purpose Machine Gun) . Giving it stacks from the gunner in the callsign . The rate of fire was sexual and comforting . Beautiful and controlled bursts .

We advanced , securing the fire support location , and waited as the contact from the head on callsign commenced . We were there . Secured the compound and safely and proficiently cleared the roof . We got our snipers up to see if they could confirm any enemy . Jerry jumped up with his 338 . A £50,000 Sniper Rifle . He started pot-shotting Taliban as they ran out the back of Crazy compound . He was standing in the standing unsupported position , and that weapons one heavy mofo so I don't think he was very successful . The target moving would of added extra difficulty to the shot .

The reason they were running out the back : because we had called in mortars and the boys from the other Patrol were dropping UGLs (Underslung Grenade Launcher rounds) in on their heads . It was mayhem . The guns were going at a good rate and at one point the commanders had to control the rate of fire . What really punctuated the attack was a missile called in from about 12 k away , straight on top of the compound . After the attack it was confirmed that there was 2 Taliban dead and who knows how many injured . In my heart it was a big ' Fuck You ' for what had happened to Gill earlier in the day and by the time we withdrew we'd been on the ground for 12 hours . I didn't want to talk to the boys about it . To be honest I didn't need to .

I had prepared myself for the absolute worst possible shit in my head and when it happened I was quite relieved that Gill was alive and well . I thought to myself he'll be fine . He'll be eating ice-cream in Birmingham with a smile on his face in a week . And he probably was . I did however here that OC was not reacting too well to what he had witnessed . OC was between Gill and I on the patrol . He was blew onto his front from the blast . OC was a G-man who was more junior than I . Respectfully . When passing him that night after everything had settled down in camp I said to him ' Hey , if you need to talk about anything about today you come into my bed space ' . I made it clear to him that I would be there for him if he needed me , and to be honest I think that reassured him . Whack sent Gill a message on Facebook a couple of days after from the FOB ,'' *Gill you'd do anything to get out of the Troop* '' . Squaddie humour . The FOB had the internet , but it was painfully slow , taking sometimes between 2-10 minutes to load a single page . But it came in handy to see how all the British fighters were doing , Khan . Froch . Haye .

An Underslung Grenade Launcher is exactly what it says on the tin . It launches grenades up to 350m away and the grenade explodes and fragments on impact . The Grenade Launcher is attached to my SA80A2 , it's underslung . The rounds go in the launcher and you take it off the safety and pull the trigger and there you go . It's an effective weapon and the Taliban hate them cause they never know where exactly they're going to land . They have a killing area of 15m from point of impact . This can alter depending on the trajectory , the ground , and where the grenade lands .

Day to day life in the FOB

We'd shit in silver-coloured bags . Seal and dump the sealed shit bag in a black industrial bag . Then burn the black bags full of our shit bags all at once . With the rest of our waste . We'd burn our rubbish and our shit bags just outside the FOB in a little incasing made of Hesco just outside the front gate and to the left . It was all done in a controlled and dignified manner . Under protection from the sanger and with one of us with our kit on , Niall the CQMS would drive the forklift out . Forks under the cages carrying rubbish . It would be dumped in the incasing and a litre of diesel thrown on it . To get the thing going .

It's no secret on Tour you do up to 3 patrols a day, fatiques (filling sandbags , heavy lifting , cleaning camp , work party's) , Admin , cleaning weapon systems , laundry (hand wash) , continue refreshing drills as they're always changing . Improving with the environment and threat level . Although the threat level in Afghan is usually always super high . It goes through the roof at poppy season . The poppy grow over a metre high and offer good cover for the enemy to contact us .

If you're lucky you'll get a nights kip of 6 hours . But depending on how many sangers need to be manned , your sleep will be rudely interrupted every night if not every other night , especially in the FOB . And then of course there's night patrols and night Op's , and this all happens 7 days a week round the clock for the duration of the Tour . It's very heavy and the longer the Tour goes on the more intense physically and mentally it gets . Wear and tear on back , knee's , elbows from constant marching , going firm , changing fire positions with uncomfortably heavy but vital kit on . Staying vigilant every time you leave the gate or on sangers has its wear and tear on your psyche . Mentally etched to respond physically and mentally at a click of the fingers , or in our case a click of the trigger from the enemy . You must be psychologically robust . This constant vigilance changes a person - if it doesn't they're not doing their job correctly or at a high enough standard .

Personally the only thing that was wrong with me was my right knee was in shit state . It was before I jumped on the plane , but I didn't want to bring any attention to it . I embraced the pain . Soldiered on . I couldn't lose my chance for Afghan . Of course my back , neck and shoulders were tight from the heavy weight carried on patrols . But these are little niggily things that a soldier has to deal with . Especially on Tour . My physique was more like a jockey's . Thin . Wiry . Strong .

Pest control

The supply to the FOB didn't help . We had a steak night in the FOB one night early in the Tour . It didn't last too long . The week after that the steak was half the size of the one the week before just so there was enough to go around . And then the week after that , no more steak night . 10 man ration boxes were cracked open . There's a variety of meals in a 10 man ration box . Meats – mince or chicken can be mixed with rice or pasta . Salt , pepper and herbs are included for flavouring . To be honest it's not bad . It's not gourmet but not bad . In each 10 man ration box there's a tin of Quaker oats and a big packet of jam – wild berry or strawberry . This little jam and porridge duo caused the boys considerable grief , especially in the PB's . In our platoon anyway . When Miller , our full bloke , realized that the boys had opened a fresh 10 man ration box just for the oats and jam , the shit hit the fan . Boys got beasted . Miller had us counting bottles of water and doing fatiques , filling sandbags , or re arranging the storeroom . He was on our cases for about 24hrs . Some of the boys were snapping . It kept us alert .

We weren't the only one's breaking into 10 mans . The mice loved the raisins and nuts that came with them and would chew right through the plastic to get to it . Cats over there are like vermin . They're not cute and cuddly . They're horrible little food thieves that would get into and could possibly contaminate our food especially in the PBs . They had to be chased away and sometimes killed as part of our daily routine . Strangled or shot was the preferred method .

When the boys were preparing food in PB South , a cat jumped up on the table out of nowhere , grabbing a steak . The little shit tried to run off with it in its mouth , but the steak was the same size as him and when chased he dropped it . The steak was ruined . How precious a prime piece of cow is when out there cannot be described . The offender was strangled and put into an industrial black bag where we put our paper plates and plastic knives and forks when we were finished eating . The little thing's neck was broke and it was still walking , moving around in this black bag in the heat of the day . We had to take him out and strangle him all over again . Talk about 9 life's . I did feel a little bit bad about that . If killing is the answer then it should be done quickly , especially to animals . But trust me , they're vermin and the place would be a cat farm if it wasn't controlled . They'd be eating our food and leaving the place very unhygienic with their urine and feces .

Applying my training

On one special day , my pre-Op training came right into play . I confirmed 2 IED's . There was 4 confirmed that day and I got 2 . The bomb disposal , better known as the EOD got the other 2 . As we progressed through our tour , the locals became more and more dependent on us . Compounds that were evacuated and left abandoned due to Taliban intimidation tactics were now being re-lived in . The intimidation tactics : the Taliban bullied owners off their land to use their compounds and fields to plant IEDs for us . Or bullying the owners of the field to grow poppy . **For them** .

213

Our job was to clear the property and surrounding areas of IED's to make it habitable for the returning owners . The first one I confirmed was in a tree line . My equipment registered high metal content and there was obvious ground sign were the land had been disturbed . There was 2 different colours of soil . The old stuff that was lighter in colour and the stuff that had been turned to cover the IED and the pressure pad . I started 6 inches back from the reading , digging down about 6 inches also , before carefully working towards it . As I got closer , the soil got softer and I neglected using fingers in favour of a fine paint brush . Eventually , after half an hour , I seen black plastic . The plastic is used to wrap round the pressure pad to preserve the wood while it's buried in the ground . I confirmed it , the EOD blew it up . When the EOD use explosives they use C4 , which is a clean explosive . If it explodes the IED's smoke will create a deafening black cloud . The explosives for the IED's in our AO are made of fertilizer and in our AO five-gallon drums were used . Filled with this explosive fertilizer . It's a dirty explosive to use .

The second IED was in front of the main entrance of the compound we were clearing . There was 2 patches of ground sign , and both had metal content readings from my equipment . I dug and uncovered the wire that was leading from the pressure pad to the drum of explosives . Again , the EOD came in and done their business . They exploded the IED with their own explosives , and not only was there a huge bolt of black smoke but it blew the two-metre high steel gates of the compound to bits . That night on the phone I suggested to Helen that I join the EOD , and before I could finish she said , ' *Well if you do we're finished* .

214

They're the ones that get blew up the most . I couldn't go through that ' . I shook off the idea but it did appeal to me , especially because they got more money .

Afghanistan as a country

Afghan is a beautiful country . It's scenic , has beautiful mountainous regions , and the wildlife is out of this world . There's some amazing birds of prey , and the coyotes come out at night . The stars are massively visible . Like sparkling diamonds on a jet black canvas . Due to the lack of light pollution . One day on stag I seen a snow leopard . It was 100m from my sentry position and was the same size as Leo , my dog . It was a cat the same size as a medium sized dog , so I put 2 and 2 together . I called it a snow leopard . I missed my dog . I missed letting him off in the parks in London with Helen and letting him chase the squirrels and pigeons . I missed Helen . I missed by baby boy . Not like miss like I shut down and don't do anything , just the day couldn't come quickly enough to see them again . Food-wise I craved a KFC fillet burger or just some standard pieces . After being solid on 10 man rations , any soldier could understand this . Could be worse . Boil in the bag . Cold . Most of all I missed Tarmac on the roads , traffic lights , cars , people who weren't trying to kill you . I just missed Western civilization . Although in and around our FOB was beautiful , with little twisty streets and paths surrounding our FOB .

The Afghan people are a common people , not like you or I. The older ones are usually village elders of their community . They all have beards . In our area of operations - we were one of the more Northerly bases and in the sticks - the people were mostly farmers . Poppy fields everywhere , although it wasn't the warm season and the fields were mostly being saturated in preparation for the summer . How can I put this eloquently : they wore long robes , we called them dish dashes and flip flops , and they didn't smell too fresh .

Right now there's over $100 Billion U.S dollars being spent on Afghan every year . They're trying to cut that figure down to 3 Billion within the next couple of years . But what is quite disconcerting is that when you ask every child , in our AO anyway , what they want to be when they grow up , they all give the same answer : ' Poppy farmer ' . Afghanies can get $20,000 U.S Dollars for one crop . In Afghan that's huge . With that money they can buy a wife . In order to have a wife the family of the girl receives a huge amount of money or farm animals , sometimes 30 cows , for the pleasure . Women are expensive all over the globe it would seem . They're Muslims so don't rule out a Poppy farmer having 2 or 3 wives and loads of kids to help with the fields . When the owner of the field dies , his eldest son gets handed the business , everything .

The Afghan kids were wild for our chocolate and hard boiled sweets from our ration boxes . We were happy to oblige . They'd follow our Patrol for a couple of hundred meters with the hope of chocolate or some boilies ' Mr , Mr , chocolate , chocolate ' . The kids would sometimes tell us where not to walk because of IED's and take us the safe routes . They were nice people and tough . Being that their climate is harsh . Really hot in the day and bitter cold at night .

Another thing we suspected they were doing was making IEDs and half sinking them . Then walking to the Base where they would make you aware of it with the hope of a small reward . We introduced a crop day were we would sell locals seed at a ridiculously low price to encourage them to produce food and not Poppy , we rationed it equally to each family so they weren't buying it cheap and selling it on at a profit . It was successful .

I said that the West of Belfast is like the wild west with their own self-appointed sheriffs , but Afghanistan takes it to another level . They are 300 years behind the Western world and with them it's who has the biggest gun and can spread the most fear rules . In Afghan that's the Taliban . I suspect it's to do with the country's lack of surrounding water . Afghanistan is geographically landlocked by 6 other countries . Iran . Turkmenistan . Uzbekistan . Tajikistan . Pakistan . China . This lack of Import-export might've kept it locked in time . Ali , our interpreter , told me that Afghanistan will never be peaceful . They need to change the name of the country . It translates to War Place . Conflict Place .

On patrol one day

On the way back from a Patrol one day I seen a village elder who was a main personality . Every time he seen our Patrol he seemed to be ganching away on his phone . Personally I suspected he was playing both sides . He was a poppy farmer , and to me he was feeding the Taliban information on our patrols and feeding us bullshit as well . I piped up on the PRR (Personal Radio) , ' Yeah I've got this bloke here , you know who he is Sir he's one of the village elders , he's on his phone , ganching away , you think he's topping it up '

AB ' Who is it big man ? '

' I don't know Sir , some fat cunt with a black beard ' . There was a trickle of laughter throughout the whole callsign .

AB ' HaHa! mad man , Go firm , I'm coming ' . AB was at the back of the patrol . I walked past this fat cunt with the black beard and looked at him sternly , advanced to the corner of the cross roads so I could see what was coming left , right and in front of me and took a knee . AB came up he had an interpreter with him and started talking away to him . Throughout the tour I became very close to AB . He was a captain and throughout my army career I'd only had one run in with him . He'd caught me with my hands in my pockets in camp one day when I was waiting for role call to be called , one cold morning back in Support Company . In the army there's no room for such conduct as putting hands in one's pockets , looking scruffy or leaning on walls . You're expected to look clean and presentable at all times . Especially in the Guards .

AB is a warm and friendly soul . He could of been a butcher or your milkman . He's just one of these guys you liked to talk to and get on with , and the locals lapped him up . He was good with people and full of charisma . On the flip side to that he was supremely confident and efficient at his job , and , to be honest , impressed the hell out of me and everybody else on that tour . He was a solid , competent operator at all times . Someone you'd trust with your life , and we did . He was a mix of Sri Lankan and caucasian , which gave him a light brown complextion , and was always sporting some crazy wolverine sidey's or some funky goatie . He was a real character and an absolute asset in the FOB .

Manneh's fate

As we put pressure on the Taliban dominated more and more of the land surrounding the FOB . In boxing perspectives you can say that the Taliban are effective counter punchers . They'll set traps , draw you on to things . What they lack in military experience they make up for in cunning , cuteness and having an indelible knowledge of their own back yard . When you hear people talking about the war in Afghan being kinetic , that's what they mean . They pull you in . We on the other hand took a more offensive come-forward approach , happy to engage with them in the pocket to meet our objective . The Taliban have been known to be that sneaky and cute that under the cover of darkness . They've been able to reverse claymores that are pointing outward , to point them back on the OPs or PBs . Facing us .

A claymore has a back blast of 15m and a killing zone of 80-100m . It's metal , like a semi-circle towards its objective , and when detonated explodes ball bearings towards its projection . If claymores are going off , the Taliban are probably trying to overrun the OP or PB . They're probably coming over the walls or trying to launch grenades in the compound . Claymores are set 10-15m out from the OP or

PB . This secures nobody will be injured in the back blast . A dense wall protecting you from the back blast allows the claymore to be placed closer . Claymore going off might indicate the beginning of a close quarter battle . The Taliban are familiar with our tactics and like a good fight . On an occasion when extracting from PB south . They held our Platoon down for 15minutes . They were hitting us from 4 different positions , effectively doing a section attack on *us* . The rounds were close but there was no casualties , and it gave everyone a buzz and something to talk about that day when we got back to the FOB .

The Company Commanders objective was to create a four sided square around the FOB with an OP at each corner manned by us . This would help to provide a safe and Taliban-free for the people who lived and existed within that square . Ultimately this objective was successful , but not without its casualties . Compounds that had either been abandoned or left would be used for these OPs . On some occasions we would pay tiny sums of money to use specific OPs if it was still inhabited by the owner .

The compounds had been made with clay and mud . When built , the mud was wet , and then hardened with time . They were durable structures . At night , compounds were snug and warm . In the day they could be quite cool . The walls were sometimes 1 foot thick . Some of the compounds we took over had little secret gardens full of fully blossomed and budding marijuana plants . We cut them down . Best not burn them . Afghan's not the ideal place to be stoned or hitting the munchies if you're Army personnel .

On New Year's Eve an Operation to secure one of these four OPs was put into action . One callsign was going to clear and control the area where the OP was going in . The other was going to go through a cleared path from the right flank to supply the materials to build the OP . I was on the second Patrol . I would be point man for the Patrol supplying the materials for this new OP . However , before we left the gate of the FOB we heard a huge explosion . I remember saying to one of the boys , ' I hope that's the fucking engineers ' . It wasn't . It was Manneh . He was on that first Patrol and he was point man . He lost two legs and an arm . His left arm at the elbow hung on by nothing but tendons and skin . It was virtually ripped off in the blast. AB was on that patrol , and a commander of the Op and the section . He tucked the limb dangling by a thread into Manneh's belt with the hope that it could somehow be salvaged as it was still attached to Manneh's body , slightly . He was loaded onto the stretcher and the Chinook took him to Bastion and then off to Birmingham .

Some fucking New Year's Eve party his wife and four children were going to have . Poor fucking Manneh . He was in the bed space opposite to me and had woke me up with his head torch that morning at about 6 . I didn't have to be up until 8 so I was a little pissed off . He lost 4 teeth as well . The explosion blasted his rifle which was slung around his front , up and into his mouth removing his top , front 4 teeth . Just 2 weeks before , we were in the sanger discussing religion . He was and still is a devoted Muslim . When waiting to leave the gate for that Op that day after the explosion , Phil Walker , who was one of our section commanders , came from the Ops room and told us it was Manneh and he'd lost two legs and an arm . He told us Manneh was in a bad way . Half an hour later we were leaving the gate to deliver the materials for our new OP . We got there , and the OP was secured when another almighty explosion occurred . This time it was an engineer , Cpl Boggie . He suffered the exact same injuries , 2 legs and one arm . It was a bad day and a very dangerous Op .

Our drills are simple . When there's a Contact IED! Apply tourniquet and FFD . In Vietnam their drills were poor . They would give the injured fluids . This is Bad drills . To stop the loss of blood it's better if the blood congeals and coagulates , restricting further blood loss from the body . Adding fluids to the body will prevent this , and a lot of injured American soldiers simply bleed out and died on the battlefield . This coagulation of blood can be aided with a low heart rate that will reduce the flow of blood around the body . So if the injured is pretty cool and calm about what's just happened , this alone can be used as a great aid .

Humour helps , or comforting words and tonality , and encouragement . When dealing with a casualty it's important to not rush in and help as there could be secondary devices . Take a kodak moment , breath , clear up to and around the casualty . Once the ground is clear give first aid , then extract and clear to the HLS and then on the Chinook and off .

My original R&R was to be for the 29th of January till the 14th of February , but I changed it with Whack for the 14th of February to the 28th , so I could spend my birthday and valentine's day with Helen . We had already booked a night at the Cotswold's . It kept me on the ground for another 2 weeks . In that time an Operation was called .

THE EARTH MOVES

On the 29th of January we got the news that there was a big Op going to happen within the next 3 days . The Taliban had repeatedly hit us over a series of 2 weeks from the same place as we left and entered our most southerly PB . It was a blatant come-on , and no other regiment had been that direction , and as far as we were intending to go . We were going to investigate . When I heard this and everyone else heard it I will be honest , there was a feeling of unpredictability and extreme danger felt within me . I can't speak for the rest of the boys . Baring in mind that we had been on Tour for 4 solid months and done countless crazy shit . I'd personally confirmed 2 IED's on the ground . That's lying flat on your belt buckle confirming , finding and uncovering IED's , first with hands followed by a paint brush . I'd fired up to 50 UGL rounds and also emptied 2 magazines of 5.56 (bullet size for an SA80A2) at the enemy , but I had a genuine feeling of " Some fucker is gona get killed if we keep doing these crazy fucking Op's " .

Flashes of being caught in an uncompromising situation , ambushed in the middle of a field with heavy machine gun fire and no cover , or taking one in the face close quarters , was etched in my consciousness , and that feeling never ever left me . I just went with it . So much so that our Battalion Priest (the Padre) , flew in to our FOB on the 30th , and on the 1st of February he conducted a mass . I prayed and ate communion like I was eating the Body of Christ . I was genuinely scared . I was elected as point man . I'd been point man for the past 2 months .

Our objective was under the cover of darkness to leave the FOB , get to the most southernly PB , which was closest to the compounds that we suspected belonged to the ones that were contacting us , take all our night vision stuff off , and set out towards the compounds at first light from the PB . We would surround the compounds and then , when the inhabitants of these compounds wake up , wish them , ' Good morning ' and introduce ourselves , simple .

One callsign went looping left and the other went looping right . I was point man of the callsign that went looping right . About 800m away from the PB I come to a tree line . AB says , ' way you go big man be careful ' . There's a path beside it . It looks chewed up and used , but for some reason I go for the tree line . It was to prove catastrophe . With my equipment I pick up a reading of metal content in the ground , but we're in the middle of bare , saturated fields used for Poppy , and the soil is a perfect , smooth carpet . Not one shred of evidence of disturbance to the ground , or that anything has been dug up and left for me . On many occasions I'd find myself digging up a stone with high metal content . I use my intuition , but before I do I look over at AB , and then I looked at Danny , right in the eyes .

Three steps later I hear a fine whistle from the earth , and then , ' **_BOOMPF!!!_** ' . The earth moves . Everything . And I'm in the middle of it all . I'm in the air . I have no control .

I'm at its mercy . Dust obscures and blinds my vision . I close my eyes . I'm spinning , once , twice , when am I going to land , half way through the second rotation I land . My body thuds against the soil and I ensue breathing like I've just run and completed my best ever pft . My breathing is fast and frantic . Before I have time to think I'm being dragged at a merciless pace out of the tree line and away from the killing area . It's AB .

At first I get a feeling like this is not happening to me . I'm not connected to what I once was . It's murky . My sense of self . Like I'm in a vessel looking out . Every particle in my body dances wildly . My skin feels euphoric . But I feel removed . I can see the dust and black smoke disperse as I'm dragged away . OC's over me ' You alright Mcgeown mucker we're gona look after you , you're alright mate , tell me about George , Little Georgie ' . At this the seriousness of the situation kicks in . I've just been hit by a fucking IED . I hope my dick and my balls are still there .

Within seconds , **' AHHH! Danny Its too FUCKIN Tight! '** . It isn't Danny it's OC . And as he cuts of the blood supply to what's left of my legs with a tourniquet , I twist in pain of my femoral artery being condensed to shear millimeters . I'm talking . I can taste explosives , dirt and debris in my mouth . I can't feel my teeth with my tongue . I wish that the chunks of dirt and debris I'm spitting out isn't my smile . I ask for water to wash my mouth out . My heads back . My ears are ringing . It doesn't register as pain . Something different . My senses vibrate . Numbness . They've taken my body armour off and I'm drifting in and out of consciousness now .

I hear AB . I hear his voice , ' McGeown tell me about George , Tell me what you think off George , Tell me about George ' . I muster all my strength ' He's ... He's ... He's fucking awesome ' . I remember 5 or 6 people around me and the Chinook's power picking up lumps of earth and flailing it wherever it pleases as it comes in . As I'm loaded onto the stretcher , my legs feel no different as I continuously kick and wave them . The boys can grab onto nothing but my bare- scorched - bones below my knees to transfer me from the ground onto the stretcher . AB gets on the Chinook with me , he's holding my hand and towering over me , ' You're a tough son of a bitch and your gona be alright , you hang on , think about George ' .

WHERE AM I , WHATS GOING ON

I woke up and panicked . I didn't know where I was . I was in a hospital , and it was late at night or early hours in the morning . Where were the boys ? Never mind , I need to do this bit by myself . My arm was wrapped up and elevated . I tried to move my fingers - Nothing . There was no one there . I was trying to get someone's attention , to comfort me I guess . So I could see how everything sits in every department . I felt weak , I was weak . My body felt wiped and punished . Like I'd been beat all over . Head . Shoulders . Arms . Especially Torso . I see a man , in the back of my head I'm still in Afghanistan and the Taliban have captured me and brought me to this place to keep me alive . It never dawned on me that the Taliban could not afford such a place . I'm talking : ' Here fella ' , a bloke small with darker complexion than average and rough black stubble . I get it in my head he's SAS and here to rescue me from this Taliban hospital , ' Here mate I'm the one , It's me , I'm the one you're looking for Irish Guards - McGeown , let's go get me out of here , bring me back to the UK ' . He comes over he tells me to be quiet . He comes close *' shhh! '.' I'm not here for you I'm here for something else '* .

' Nah mate your here for me get me out of here'

' shhh! You're in the UK '

' Where ? '

' *Birmingham* '

I don't believe him as I try to stay awake and alert for another 30 minutes . And then I fall asleep . I'm very tired . I'm weak . I fall asleep thinking that the man is lying to me and I fall asleep hoping that the Taliban do not have a change of heart in the middle of the night and be-head me as I sleep . I am very weak and vulnerable and they could do what they want with me . The next day I wake it's night again or again early hour's in the morning . I can hear some automatic burst in the background and see the flash of the huge machine gun 1000m over my right shoulder . They're defending their prizes inside and I'm one of them . This time I stay awake for 2 hours and realize that I could be in a UK hospital . Everything seems a bit clearer now , but I still hope that the Taliban don't see my shape and profile through the glass window and slot me in the back while I'm sitting up in my bed . I dose off again .

When I wake up it must be early in the day . A nurse sees me looking at her ; she's lovely and approaches me ; she talks to me with gentleness and care . I notice that I can't talk ; there's something in my throat . I look down . There's a tube . My automatic response is to pull it out . I do and its massive . I keep pulling in disbelief at how much of this tube as entered my body , some white stuff comes out with the tube as the last of it comes out . The nurse has turned while this is all happening to get some assistance . The doctor comes . She's about 30 , blonde and pretty , ' *That tubes going to have to go in again* ' , are the first things out of her mouth . The first thing out of mine is , ' That tubes not going back in my fucking mouth , what the fuck was that! ' .

' We've been feeding you through that tube for the last 2 days ' , she looks at me like that's supposed to mean something

' Well it's not going in again , fucking forget about it! '

She looks at me like I've ruined her tea party ' Well then it's solids ' , she says it in a ' like you've left me no other choice ' tone of voice .

' Fuck it then , Yeah Whatever ' .

A couple of hours later the menu comes out for the food . I looked at it . It all seemed a bit limited for the UK , but the Salmon and mashed potato caught my eye and so I ordered it . When it came out , the Salmon was still the same shape of the tin it had just come out of and the potatoes were extremely lumpy . Straight away I was like , ' I'm not fucking eating that ' , I was expecting a fresh piece of salmon straight from the Scottish Highlands that was caught the morning before , and steamy warm full mashed potato with a bit of parsley on top . I said to the nurse , ' Why the fucks the food so shit ? ' . She said ' the food has to be sterile so you don't get any infections . This is the food you have to eat in the ICU ' , [Intensive Care Unit] , ' It's that or the tube ' . What is it with these people and that fucking tube . They're fucking obsessed . ' Alright I'll eat it ' I said , as I accepted I had no other choice than to do so . Every bite I ate was casually observed by the 30 year old doctor from a distance while she was doing her admin . Every bite was painful because it was disgusting , and I drank and gulped with each bite to wash it down . I looked at the doctor as I ate , " You fucking Bitch . Try and stick that tube down my throat ". I finished 3/4 of it . I was happy with my performance . I thought I'd stick the charm on . ' I'll eat it all next time . Taking me a while to getting my throat used to swallowing again . Thank You ' . She documented everything that I'd left on the plate .

Later on that day a couple of the boy's from the Irish Guards welfare team came in . They shook my hand and it was good to see them . Do you want to see Helen , your brother's here as well . I was elated . ' Yeah of course , where are they ? ' . George was there , my eldest brother Greg stayed with him as Helen came in to see me . George was 6 months old and I didn't want him to see me in this state . Helen came in to see me . She looked good , ' Oh Colum what have you done to yourself , you're a mess , you silly boy ', I loved her honesty . ' I know , I'm sorry , I'll make it up to you . So Greg's here ? '

' Sean as well '

' Fucking hell , Sean as well '

Sean is my younger brother . When my brother Greg left the family house , Chris had the biggest bedroom upstairs all to himself and the 3 below him in age , were jammed into a bedroom that had just been halved because of the arrival of my little sister , and a partition wall going up to create a new room for her . I was 16 , a week away from my 17th birthday and I was sharing a bedroom with my 14 and 12 year old little brothers Sean and Brendan . I was angry . I was angry about living in a bedroom with my 2 younger brothers , sharing bunks . I was angry that my older brother had a bedroom to himself that was bigger than the one I was in and that I had to share with 2 kids that were younger than me and had been doing all my fucking life . I hated that my father had cancer and my mother was telling me and everyone else in the house to , ' tip toe round your father because he's had a dose of chemo and he's nervy ' . Give a bull in a china shop an excuse . I was angry that this seemed to be going on for years and it genuinely seemed ALL one way and it wasn't for me or my favour . I hated my Auntie's - my father's sister's coming over and chastising us and saying , ' can you not just do what your father asks of you ' , and when you replied that it didn't make a bit of difference because he would find something to be angry with anyway and then when you didn't agree with them they would say ' You know what your problems are yous are all spoilt ' . Are you taking the piss lets change positions for one day and you live under this roof with that nightmare as one of his children for 24 hours . The last thing you would call me ever again would be spoilt . You fucking jokers .

I hated being in the middle and never getting any favours , I was neither the eldest or the baby . And I took it out on my brother's one day both of them it was wrong and I was very violent with them . They were just kids . I'm sorry . And then give a bull in a china shop an excuse . My father was equally and then surpassed what I had done on my brothers by a milestone . He punched me out of the bedroom , down the stairs , the length of the hallway , out the door and 10-15 m up the street before my mother did her little party trick of pulling him of one of us . It just so happened to be me this time . I purposefully walked as slow as I could as all this was going on to show nothing but utter contempt for the man , his punching power , his everything . I was going to walk out that house in my own good time and slowed down the pace so he could get better shots at my face to cement the lack of power he had over me physically or mentally .

It resulted in about 50 unanswered punches to the head . As he whizzed around me pulling me , holding and pushing me into position for better angles for which him to land his arsenal . I was so far gone with living in that house that death was a more pleasant option and that wasn't going to happen anytime soon . And from that day on it was a rare occasion that Sean and I ever crossed paths and if we did it was brief and uninspiring . He was an academic genius with a loving way and soft nature and I was the complete opposite . He worked on a chemist on the road and my mother once told me that the people that worked in the chemist could scarcely believe that Sean and I came from the same mother . I don't blame them we might of looked like polar opposites . And here he was over to see me .

3 days ago I was in Afghanistan with my brother's in arms , my family , and now this young man who I gave a torrid time to when I was younger is here supporting me . It was overbearing and when I seen him I couldn't contain it , my feelings , my emotions , my new state of complete

vulnerability , my loss of limbs of which I hadn't even lifted the blanket yet to look at , I was waiting for the right moment . And I was sorry , he didn't live locally he had jumped on a plane to see me . I didn't think he cared and I wouldn't of held it against him if he didn't . I was an angry kid back then and unfortunately for both of us he seemed to be there . Again , Sorry Sean for all that . This fight I mentioned was the catalyst for me entering my grandfather's home the first time . This was the huge fight I talked about at the end of the sixth chapter .

That afternoon when everyone had left , I was strong and ready to look at what had happened . I'd took a sneak peak at my dick and balls but wouldn't go any further . I psyched myself for the worst , steadied myself and lifted the sheets . My right leg was all but gone but 3 inches and at this stage my left knee and knee cap were still attached . ' Gleaming , Fuck it , let's go ' , I said to myself . Let's get the fuck out of this ICU . I was told by the welfare officers that on that next ward you could get any scoff you wanted and visitors at any time of the day and even go out for a McDonalds . McDonalds was stinking . I wanted a steak , blue , with a pint of Guinness . 2 days later I charmed , talked and smiled my way out of the ICU .

MY PARENTS

My father is one of the toughest , hardest men I've ever met . What I witnessed him do physically year after year for decades is a testament to his physical and mental toughness , drive and focus . His work rate was phenomenal for years and to be around a man like that . Let's just say when you put your hand in a honey jar some of it can't help but stick . Of course he was an influence in my life . But I only ever tried to take the good attributes from his personality and sieve out the rest . I would look at some of these so called hard men in my neighbourhood with their reputations . To be honest they weren't a hundredth of the man my father was . Not even close . It was embarrassing . My father's beat cancer several times , maybe three . And since he was diagnosed he does a swim for Marie Curie every year . He's been doing that swim for about 15 years now . And it wouldn't be unheard of for him to swim up to a mile in one sitting for this charity .

My mother met my father when she was 16 . They courted each other for a couple of years and then when my father was around 21 he went to Australia for 14 months . He worked on the roads laying concrete pipes and when he came back he had enough money to afford a down payment on his first house . My mother waited for him but when he came back he'd drunk that much beer and had a ginger beard that my mother scarcely recognised him at the airport . They married soon after .

When we were kids she was given £100 a week for shopping to feed two adults , 6 kids and my grandfather . She was amazingly resourceful . At times she would go without a potato or a piece of meat just to put it on our plates . She's a good woman , my mother .

Years went past . I would observe my mother when she would be washing the dishes or peeling potatoes at the sink . She would sing this song . 'I beg your pardon I never promised you a rose garden' , she sang it with such sadness that it wasn't hard to imagine that whatever her rose garden was , she never got it . It was moments like these that I seriously questioned my role , my very existence , in that house . But what was promised to her was mountains of washing , and maintaining a house , with 5 pro-active kids all living their own lives and doing their own thing .

When my father was a boy it was in the ages were the headmaster or the teacher would give you 10 of the best , with a belt or metre long ruler . I guess we got a little bit of the same treatment , from him . And coming from west Belfast which had been and still was from my experience a rough , violent place with working class grit and toughness , and a political cesspool that made for a predatory and fearful place for any youngster growing up there . I'm happy I experienced it . I grew up quickly .

I didn't witness the Troubles of the late 60's early 70's , but what I did witness was the aftermath even many years later . A generation who had been pushed and pulled morally , physically and psychologically by the whole events , and , like a great tsunami , the damage was done and I missed its destruction but there was always a feeling in the air that I was living in a more peaceful era , than the one before . What could be salvaged from the wreckage **was** salvaged , and it was time to move on .

My mother and father have an obsession with death and sickness . They're always talking about who has cancer , who had cancer , who's dying of cancer , who just died of cancer , or , has recently passed away . My brothers sleg him that he plans his week around the funerals he'll be attending that week . I actually can see where they're coming from . It's crazy but seems like common practice in working class Belfast . He was cut up about the whole thing . I don't think I've ever witnessed an emotional response from my father apart from when his mother died . I recently met up with him and he said I was always trying to outdo people , ' Most people stand on dog shit , you had to go and stand on an IED ' , Typical . He's a small , stout , stocky man who reminds me of Phil Mitchell from Eastenders .

TIME TO HEAL

I got my arse upstairs and got wheeled into a room with 3 other boys . It was a four man room . And it was like something out of the land of the living dead . There was 2 doubles and a triple . When they wheeled me in , the energy in the room was that morbid I pulled the curtains around my bed space , or got the nurses to . I was in the bed close to the window , and whatever way the variety of window panes were shaped , the guy across from me thought I was looking at him in the reflection of the windows . He was a double and he had his girlfriend with him . She was a pretty little thing . But a bit too much . The outfit she was wearing was very revealing and her tits and ass were hanging out . To be honest I just got blew up 5 days ago and hadn't seen my son in 4 months the last thing I wanted to do was look at anyone . I just wanted to be left alone and I had this fucker across the way giving snide comments about me staring at him . ' Mate I don't know what you think you're seeing in that reflection but believe me I'm not fucking looking at you ' . I felt like saying , ' Who the fuck are you , I'd wana look at you ' . I didn't wana be negative to him or ruin his morale .

But eventually the other 2 joined in , ' *Yeah don't worry about it mate we've got your back , we'll get him when he's sleeping* ' , about me . It was fucking unreal . How the fuck is 2 doubles and a triple gona get me , spit on me . It was fucking bizarre . At that I had to pipe up ' Mate none of yous are gona do anything , I know what yous are doing , Fucking knock it on the head , What are you gona do ? We're all in fucking clip , You're not gona do anything so knock it in the head ' . It continued . 13 hours later the nurse came in . She'd been in and out trying to defuse the situation . ' Listen I don't wana be here in this room with this energy , Get me the fuck outta here ' . Half an hour later I was in a 1 man room by myself . I felt better . It was dark . I looked out the window . I could see lights , tarmac on the roads . Traffic lights , fucking traffic lights I was in the Great British Empire again . I could see it but I couldn't feel it . My heart was still out with the boys , just wishing that I would be the last one in this predicament .

What was left of my legs was bruised and my groin area was green and blue with bruising . There was a 2 inch shrapnel wound on my right arse cheek . My arm was still wrapped up and my torso sides were raw . They'd been stripped of a layer of skin for skin graft for my right arm and my left leg . I couldn't get out of bed and so every time I needed a shit I would have to buzz . It was humiliating .They would slip a little cardboard cup under my arse and then wipe my arse for me . Every move I made was painful . My body was in rag . 4 months in Afghanistan and then getting blew up is traumatic to the body .

Every morning I would have to peel my sheets off my sides . My arm was slowly improving and the morphine was a constant . When I looked at what was left of my limbs they were wrapped tight and I didn't know what was beneath the wraps . It sounds ridiculous but I was afraid to lift them in case they fell off . I thought that under that wrap was a Frankenstein job , were my left leg had actually been sewn back on . Pure pride and not wanting these nurses constantly cleaning up after me and wiping my arse every time my bowels moved increased my recovery . There was little machines on my arm and legs that literally sucked all the shit and dirt that had been blown into the wounds from the explosion . They worked around the clock . And what came out looked like a jam rolly-polly , with a bit of chocolate in there for good measure . It was the blood , puss , filth and dirt and any other infectious materials that my body was getting rid of . They were like 3 little mini dysons . I had an operation to remove my knee cap . They put me to sleep and when I woke up it felt like I'd been violated . My soul felt soiled . The pain was immense and like nothing I'd ever felt before . Within 5 minutes they'd given me a cocktail . Half an hour later I didn't have a worry in the world . It was 10 days since I got blew up and I was feeling much better .

Top of the world actually . Helen came into the room she had some shampoo . I could still smell the explosives on my hair , the cordite , it was like cling film in my hair . I washed it out with the help of Helen and some little nurse . It was time to see George : I hadn't seen him in so long . I was wheeled into the Tv room , it was quieter . He was massive . My big boy . I couldn't hold him , my arm was still fragile , a couple of my tendons were damaged in the blast and had to be tied together . I gave him a kiss and went back to my room and I just knew I was going to smash this little recovery period as quickly as humanly possible . I have a boy there I've been apart from most of his life . I need to get out of here and start being a daddy . Let's get these legs

. I had no idea what I was going to do career wise . Somewhere in the back of my head I knew my Army career was over . I looked out of the window . I'm in the Uk . I'm safe . I could see the cars and the tarmac and the buildings . I slept knowing that I was going into the unknown but I had a reason to go on . I had George . I had everything .

The attention I got in the Queen Elizabeth was next to none and the specialist after specialist coming in and out of my room on a half an hour basis was so impressive I was in awe . I couldn't help but get better . A huge flux of Irish Guards came in it to see me . It was great . I was jovial and upbeat and enjoyed performing as they came in . AB came in ; it was great to see him . He was on R&R . He looked , dare I say , a little guilty . I didn't notice , but Helen said after , ' He looked awful ' . I was just happy to see my good friend . It lifted me no end . Thanks AB . For my 27th birthday I went to Frankie and Benny's with Jarvis and his family who came to see me . The drinks were on the house courtesy of the MLOs (Military Liaison Officers) . I had a steak , blue , and a Jack Daniels and coke . It was a great birthday . I was happy to be alive . Dave kell being from Birmingham , his mother Mary Francis came to visit me . I'd never felt so much unconditional love and reassurance as I did from her . Thank you Mary Francis you were there for me tremendously . I don't think I can ever repay you . Again , Thank you .

4 weeks after I was blew up I was starting my rehab at Headley Court . The Queen Elizabeth said it was one of the quickest recoveries in 5 years . Thank You QE : my recovery was so quick due to your professionalism , love and care .

HEADLEY COURT HERE I COME

I came from the QE straight to Headley Court after taking a one weekend break at the Malmaison Hotel in Birmingham . When I was there the Aston Villa Football Team were staying at the same time . They were rowdy . I had a good meal and spent the first night in 5 months with Helen . We had a cot and George wouldn't sleep , not a wink ; he just kept making a little clicking noise to let his mummy and daddy know he was still awake . It was so cute . He was 7 months old . It must of been the excitement of finally meeting this ' Daddy ' that mummy had been talking about nearly all his life . I was on medication and my core temperature would fluctuate out of control . My body temperature would soar massively and at night the sheets would be drenched with fluid leaking from my pours . My body for 26 years produced 8 pints of blood but with this new injury of me missing my right leg and half of my left . It took a while for my body to register this new required amount of blood needed . A lesser amount was needed within my body because of the loss of limbs and the excess blood being pumped around my body increased my temperature to unusually high levels . I had tablets for everything . Some of them were making me feel a little stoned . I didn't like taking them . On the other hand others were controlling this new ' phantom pain ' . I was basically receiving masses amounts of pain to my legs even though I didn't have them anymore , and it took over 6 months for my brain to process that they don't actually exist anymore . I could feel cramps and shooting pain in my legs and feet that weren't even there , very vividly . Sometimes the pain was over bearing . Keep you up nights sort of pain .

Some of the guys I met in Headley court with the same injuries had suffered shattered or damaged back , lower back , pelvis or hips . I was very lucky when I got hit : I was 10½ stone and took off like a rocket . I was maybe 11¼ stone when I left the UK . A lot of the guys with these injuries were much heavier and took the blast with more impact because of their weight . I was simply in it . And got threw away from it . I was very lucky I landed on my back . Some guys land on their heads . Sometimes their heads open like coconuts . When that happens , very unpleasant , very bad and neurological damage can surely follow .

On a scale of the worst possible shit that could of happened to me . 100% being a slow agonizing or quick death , 20% of it came true . I'm lucky I'm not a triple amputee , my right arm was so badly damaged there was talk of lobbing it off . That's horrific . That would of brought the scale up to 40% . Dick and balls gone 60% . Eyes gotta be up in the 80%s . Continuing my life in the dark . That's tragic . I'm very lucky . Some people lost their balls and pieces of their tackle , some get their arse cheeks blown off . One bloke I remember in the QE looked like he'd been cut in half , a Gurkha , nothing from the hips down . And a lot of peoples progress was haltered because their open wounds got infected and they received what was widely known in Birmingham as the ' Afghan bug ' . The dirt and shit from the field and the Taliban have been known to shit and urinate on the IEDs or around them for this reason . Those first few QE days I meditated and could feel my body push out and reject the dirt that had entered it . I focused on my body cleansing itself with the aid of those little mini dysons .

I got settled into Headley court . The first 6 weeks in Headley are solid . My OT (Occupational Therapist) Belinda was not happy about sending me back the first weekend . She had read the reports and said something about the wound on my arse . I think my response was something along the line of , ' *I don't give a fuck what you think , You haven't even looked at my arse and I haven't seen my dog in 5 months* ' . I had not seen my dog in so long and I missed Leo dearly . Helen told me he pined for 4 months when I left . I am sorry about that Belinda .

What I missed was looking into my dog's eyes and having a big cuddle of unconditional love . George was 2 months old and had a wonderful mummy . The dog and I had a deeper connection . After a week in Battalion there's nothing I enjoyed more than going to the Park and watching him run and bicker with the other dogs . Watching him run reminded me that I didn't have to and that I was somewhat in my own time . Leo was like my eldest son . He was a year old when I rocked up with Helen and his behaviour was dreadful the first 6 weeks , always in the Park , my arrival threw him off kilter . But after that initial rough patch we were best buds . He was clever and very sensitive . A great family dog . Our bond was strengthened one boxing day when he was attacked by a Pit Bull and some American looking Fighting Dog . The woman walking them coolly let us know what was going to happen , ' *Oh watch the small one , He's very domineering you know* ' . ' Why have they got muzzles on ' , I replied with a look suggesting if they're aggressive missus they shouldn't be off the lead . Muzzles isn't the answer for a vicious dog . Correctional training is .

Before we knew it , all Hell broke loose . Both muzzles were knocked off both dogs in the carnage . The woman sat back , not getting involved while her Pit lock jawed onto Leo's front forearm . Leo locked onto the American's bottom jaw as I proceeded to punch the head of the Pit . Me being so tall . The Pit being so small , my punching downwards at his Tyrannosaurus Rex head had no real effect . My fist bounced of his head . The woman stood there still not involved like it was all in a day's work for her two Champions . That all changed when I repeatedly jumped and tried to snap the Pit's back with my Feet . Stamping on his back as hard as I could . She kindly got involved then . £220 vet bill , antibiotics for a week and a lamp shade on his head for 2 weeks to stop him licking his wounds . He was hang dog for a while but recovered eventually . I was proud of him . He stood his own and it was like we both fought those two little bullies together .

So there you go , I missed my dog more than my newly born son , but it was only because I knew the pivotal role I played in Leo's daily life . I knew he would pine for me , and I also knew that if I never came back from Afghan Helen would do a wonderful job with George and give him a wonderful childhood . This connection to Leo , along with me being lifted off my feet , every particle in my body being exploded 10ft in the air and dumped in a field in Afghan with all the boys - I guess I was still a little raw from the whole incident ; so again Belinda , I was in the wrong , Sorry .

4 weeks into Headley court I got some terrible news that 2 Irish Guards had been killed . It was Major Matt Collins and Lsgt Mark Burgen , better known to his friends as Burgo . It was tragic ; they were 3 days from coming off the ground when their vehicle was hit by an IED . They were killed instantly . I have fond memories of Major Collins ; he was my Company Commander when I was in Support Company with the snipers . He was on the ground when I got hit and held my drip for me while the Chinook came in . I don't need to say it , he was a man of massive integrity , a fine man with huge admiration and belief in his boys . An asset to any fighting group not just for his soldiering capability but his professionalism and morale he brought to the team . It was an honour and pleasure to work for him in Support Company and he will be dearly missed by the Battalion and the men who served beneath him . I only had ever encountered Burgo once and it wasn't in Battalion .

When Helen was 6 months pregnant we went to Tunisia for a week it turned out to be 2 because of the volcanic ash cloud . We went to a place in Tunisia called El Gem . It was beautiful , with olive trees everywhere . Fields of them , some of them 2 thousand years old and still producing olives . We visited an Amphitheatre where Gladiators used to battle , and bang in the middle of that Amphitheatre Burgo and I bumped into each other . He was with his partner and I was with mine . He said ' Hi ' , I said , ' Alrite ' and we continued doing what we were doing . I never knew him that well , but some of the boys , especially the signals Platoon , were absolutely heart broke . Our thoughts are with you and your family Burgo and the fiance you left behind , Always . When I heard the news and who it was that was killed I instantly went off my medication . It was numbing me out and I felt quite ill at hearing the news . I attended the funeral for Major Matt Collins . It was a beautiful mass .

In Headley I came across someone that I regard as a Dear friend . He is the best physio in Headley . His name is Pete and I like to call him ' The Major ' , because that's his rank . At first he seemed too keen in my opinion ; I thought he seen everyone as a future Olympian . I had to slow him down a bit . What he wanted from me and what he was actually going to get at this stage in my rehab was like black and white . Two different ends of the spectrum . The way I slowed him down , you guessed it , talked incessantly , about anything , life , Afghan , me back in Battalion , philosophy , poems or quotations that I had read .

After a week with him , and him seeing that things weren't exactly going his way . I let the Major know that walking was the last thing on my mind . It was . I was only out of Afghan for a month , had one weekend off coming from the QE , and then had come straight to Headley . I explained to him that I didn't know when the last time was when I read a book or basically sat around and done nothing or had some time to myself . I wasn't ready for a surge of activity . And anyway , the first set of little legs I got , you can use the politically correct term ' stubbies ' . That's what all the cool folks at Headley Court call them - I would take three steps and fall on my face . That happened for the first 5 weeks . It was very frustrating , and until they added 2cm on my right stubbie this continued . All of a sudden , after this little adjustment being done , my foot is hitting the ground at the right time and I'm off .

Stubbies class is exactly what it says on the tin . It's a class were you work on different skill sets on your stubbies , walking side to side , walking backwards , picking things up . I'll never be able to do the moonwalk again , but then I never could before the incident but with stubbies ; I could do a bit of line dancing , side to side , spin , clap , Yeo! .

In stubbies class we were told to have a tug of war on a blue mat . Initially it was hard enough to keep your balance on solid , level flooring , the mat adds extra balancing complications because its soft . I watched some of the other boys doing it , and the ERI's were in stitches laughing . I was asked to participate next . I reluctantly agreed to . Again , I was fresh in and didn't want to be starting off on the wrong foot so to speak ... I was falling all over the place without being pulled , and after 3 times falling I called time . They'd had their fun out of me . 6-7 weeks ago I was on the front line with the boys fighting for the boys and to provide for my newly born son George and my beautiful , educated partner Helen . I'm a proud man . But now I'm providing amusement not through any intellect but by falling over uncontrollably on some blue mat while some other bloke in the same situation tries to beat me in a tug of war . I didn't like this , right from the beginning , and it didn't exactly do wonders for my self-esteem . Didn't damage it , but certainly didn't boost it , and I was only determined to do exercises and spend my energy in activity that would directly benefit my progress . Next time I was asked to do stubbies class I vented my opinion ' I'm not doing this . It's fucking ridiculous . I'm a grown man and I have a little boy back in London ' , I walked away .

After that I ripped through my whole timetable . A lot of it was just some stranger who'd never met me filling in the gaps . Sometimes there was up to 3 hours of phis a day ; I don't need to do 3 hours phis a day . I was a very well-conditioned soldier . Some of the guys unfortunately probably did need this 3 hours a day as a lot of them ballooned in weight , too many Dominos pizzas , too much alcohol consumption , and being advised like I was to increase my calorie intake to over seven thousand calories a day because C-legs (Computer Legs) use 3 times more energy to power than walking with natural limbs . This perhaps wasn't the best advice to give the boys . The average daily calorie intake for a man is 2550 . I think I'd be violently ill if I tried to put 7000 calories in my skinny frame .

Walking with just your right arse cheek and the other side being through-knee . I'm thankful for that length on my left . It's were all my power comes from . The more of a lever you have the easier it is to walk . The more you can do . It takes about 6 months for your body to settle down and to readjust your balance . In one of our little meetings with the doc they referred to my levers as stumps . I stopped them , ' I don't like that word , don't say it again , I prefer the term residual limbs , levers , or plain old legs ' . Even though I had an inside joke with Helen that my right side looked like a little docked boxers tail .

I started doing my own phis , powering through the swimming pool , fast explosive lengths with short recovery period . I knew what I was aiming for . The best way to walk on stubbies is not in stubbies class but loads and loads of practice during the day , guided by the Major . I will give stubbies class its dues : it did teach me a couple of basic skill sets . But the bulk of my progress came from the Major , Cheers Pete .

Meeting the Celtic warrior

One day word got around that Captain Buckley and Captain Wilmont had Steve Collins coming to see all the Irish Guards at the local pub . It was true . It was great to see him and when I sat down I instantly started talking about him and his career . The 2 fights each with Chris Eubank and Nigel Benn . He was incredibly open about his experiences in the ring and bought us all a steak dinner and as many drinks as we wanted . I left having complete admiration for the guy for his humbleness and generosity . A true character and back in the day for about 3 and ½ years an unbeatable warrior at super middleweight .

Steve Collins for me and a lot of other boys in Headley is a Great inside and out of the ring . A real diamond with a massive heart . Steve doesn't do things in half measures . He and a team that work for him funded 19 wounded servicemen on an unforgettable trip to Las Vegas . Visiting the casinos , the Grand Canyon , and staying exclusively in The Bellagio Hotel . He pulled strings for this . Steve brought a lot of business to the Strip when he fought as a middleweight in his earlier days . You bring the Irish and the American Irish to the Strip . They spend money . Everyone's happy .

He did this through the charity he founded . Polo For Heroes . Trips like these are very beneficial . Especially for the younger guys who get hit . It speeds up the recovery process ; it's a positive experience and can be used for a spring board for the new version of you .

No soldier , injured or not , deserves the energy and attention and input that Steve has given us . He's so down to earth , so real and so intense that , when meeting him up close and personal it's easy to see why he achieved what he did in the squared ring . Again Steve , from myself and the other service men . Thank You .

Reuniting with old friends

It was at this stage that I realized that Helen and I were over as an item . I seemed to be conserving all my energy to handle and survive Helen at the weekend . She was not coping well with the transition . I don't blame her . In fact . I admire her for her honesty , strength and courage for making it clear that she could not cope with this change in her life . 6 months before , I was this fit more than capable animal who could carry anything on his shoulders both physically and mentally ; and now - well , now I was in the Ice Age were we walked on all fours , and having to learn all over again . It was a difficult and challenging time . I had two options . One was doing nothing in Headley and conserve all my strength for the weekend with Helen . Or two , Say goodbye to Helen and focus on my rehab , because it had to be done anyway . I chose the latter of the two and my rehab went through the roof . It felt like a weight had been lifted off my shoulders . My brother in London let me sleep on his couch for 3 months until I got my own place . I'm very thankful to him for that . In and around this time the Battalion had come back , and Chris Tobin came into London to see me . We went to O'Neills bar in Clapham , and the drinks were on me .

We sat down and Chris , being at the point of the patrol that day , with myself would be able to tell me what happened and everybody's role in it all . He told me it was a cold morning and the noise of the IED echoed through the cold air . It must have been like an alarm clock to the Taliban , as up until then it was a covert operation . They contacted the Chinook with automatic burst from small arms fire as it took off with me in it . The reason there was no ground sign is because it rained heavy the night before we deployed on the ground for this Op . A vital part of information I failed to register . Though it could have been there 6 months before I stood on it . This is what's known as a legacy IED , left that long that it's long forgot about . There's hundreds if not thousands of legacy IED's in Afghanistan waiting to be trod on by locals or Army personnel .

After 4 months on the ground , my senses were more frayed and I'd been shot at that many times and had that many safe escapes it left me stubborn and bull-headed in my approach that day . When you're 2 months away from your R&R , you're still loco about the job and the way you're doing it , but when you're 2 weeks away , loco becomes ballsy and brave . There's light at the end of the tunnel . 2 months away , the days flowed , but 2 weeks away from R&R each day felt like a long week . And along with that the Ops were becoming more ballsy and daring . We weren't slowing down , we were building and trying to compound our interest on our investment .

The day I got hit , I had 20 UGL rounds in my pouch and a Lazum on my back . It's a mini Rocket Launcher which is accurate up to 150m and costs £4,000 . There was UGL rounds everywhere and they couldn't find the Lazum that was attached to my back . One of the trees in the tree line was felled and there was a huge crater in the ground . Chris told me that when I got blew up my bowels opened and I shit myself . There was shit and blood everywhere . I do remember the runs being rife in camp that week . It must have been messy . Chris applied countless FFDs (First Field Dressings) to me , and was complaining that I had ruined his Gucci gloves . Gucci kit is expensive kit that soldiers purchase out of their own pocket . He'd had them since Iraq , for 4 years , and had to dump them when he got back to the FOB that day .

I was lucky : the night before , a blast-proof nappy was threw on my bed . When I got blew up the nappy which is clipped around your belt was removed with the blast in the process . Me being a skinny little white kid from Belfast everything fitted in the nappy just fine , if you get what I mean . However , if my name was big bad Leroy Brown from the Caribbean , I'm sure it would have been hard to tuck everything in . It was a tight fit and saved my dick and

253

balls . I was the first person to get blew up with that piece of equipment on . Somebody up there loves me .

It was then that I decided that It was time to wheel my arse into Battalion and see the boys . So I did , the next day . When I got there they were all getting ready for the big wedding . Prince William and the Duchess of Cambridge were getting married , and the Irish Guards were street-lining for the big day . We really are a fine Regiment . Four weeks earlier we'd been fighting Taliban .

The boys from 2 company joined me in the local and wouldn't let me put my hands in my pocket . It was great to see them and very overwhelming . I spent that night in Windsor with Chris and his girlfriend , and the next morning his girlfriend dropped me off at the station in Windsor to get the train to Waterloo and then Charing Cross . It was the first time that I'd ever felt apart from the Battalion , left behind .

I got to my brothers flat , he was at work , went into his bedroom and cried uncontrollably for about half an hour . I felt an emptiness and my lungs felt cold and wet . The Battalion went on to practice drill for the big wedding and I was dropped off at the train station by myself . It was a harsh reality that my army career was over and the British army had no more use for this wounded lion . I was a soldier with no use to anyone . I spent the rest of the day in bed trying to make sense of my life and what I was good for . The fact that I was alive and could contribute to George's life physically and financially gave me hope . I didn't stay down for too long and the next day I'd pulled myself together .

Realisation things certain things have changed

I would of at least did another 4 years , I believe I would
have done half a service – 12 years , jumped on a couple of
promotion courses and then left to open that burger van or
be close to my growing son . I got my HGV just before I
deployed so I could drive some of the armoured vehicles ,
so that was a little bit of a backup . I would of loved to do a
South African close protection course , Ronin . With the
intention of working only in the UK to be there for my son .
But like everyone this probably would not of happened and
I would have had to go where the money was , Middle East
. Helen and I would still be together ; in fact the injury was
the catalyst for us parting . I never knew it but the second I
stood on that IED the relationship was effectively over , it
just took a couple of months for me to realize it . Although I
say this Helen was hugely supportive at the beginning , I
felt . I got compensated for the injury .

In fact I had a dream 3 months after moving into my new
place . A ground floor flat . I was 5 minutes away from my
euthanasia and the clock was ticking . I was smoking crack
and in complete bliss . For the record I haven't got the first
clue about crack but it is a dream . I had this overpowering
feeling that the world , George and everyone else on the
planet would be better off from my euthanasia . The only
person who was going to miss anything was me . I felt a
sadness that I was putting this life to death even though
the dream was so vivid and joyous because of it . My death
could only do George good . Euthanasia - ending one's life .
And when I woke I was in pure peace . I was no longer

struggling , no longer fighting , I had in fact escaped my working class-roots . I escaped it in the most extreme and surprising circumstances , but escaped it nonetheless .

This is how I interpreted the dream : putting the working class boy to death . He is no more , but of course there are facets of my personality that will always remain . I can no longer walk into a room , a bar , a setting and know that physically I'm the main man . I just can't . I have no feet but I'm proud of the journey I've taken and the difference I felt I may have made , I think however long my life lasts I might find happiness .

It's easier to except and injury like this when you've excepted death so many times in your life . Every time I got into a fight in Andytown I was fighting till the death . To put a life and death emphasis on any situation brings you to a heightened state of what the body , mind and psyche can achieve . I remember a story about my two cousins who lived in the country , they're names are Kevin and Dan . They were goofing around on a sit down lawnmower , this lawnmower is a heavy industrial piece of machinery weighing half a tonne . Dangerous thing to be goofing around on , and this day proved to be very dangerous indeed . Whatever happened a kid from the neighbourhood jumped on it and accidently ran over my cousin Kevin , completely over him . He was lucky he wasn't chewed up into bits , but the back of his head and back had bad lacerations , deep lacerations . He was a very very lucky boy . The point of the story is that when he was under it and the engine had been stopped his younger brother Dan lifted this piece of machinery at one side . He was 13 years old and lifting this ½ a tonne piece of machinery , he was pleading with his brother

' Kevin Kevin you need to pull yourself out I don't know how much longer I can hold this '

Kevin did manage to pull himself out , his clothes were ripped off his back and stained red with blood . He suffered severe lacerations and lost a lot of blood . When met with death , death to yourself or death to somebody you hold dear the human body can have insurmountable strength . This story just validated everything I already knew , even from a young age . I was dead jumping on that plane to Afghan and I came back missing a piece or two of myself , but I came back alive and as long as you're breathing there's hope .

New York New York

An opportunity to go to New York came up with Help for Hero's – BattleBack , and I jumped on it . BattleBack is funded by Help for Heroes . As it was in America , America's Wounded Warriors were our host , and I had an unforgettable time . We arrived into DC for the first 3 nights . Everyone was lovely and very friendly . Especially the women . We visited the White House . We got a private jet 3 days in from DC to New York where we handbiked all over the place , visited Ground Zero , The Brooklyn Bridge , which was partly closed so we could cross it , before driving to the Hamptons . We had a mega party in the Hamptons and sailed out to Fire Island for another party . It was great . We ate and drank like kings and the Americans made their country look beautiful . They're a very patriotic country and really admire their wounded for the sacrifices they've made . America ticked all the boxes . And 10 days later we all came back . I was in Awe , and felt bigger and stronger . It was a great experience . I needed to do this for closure with Helen and to move on with the rest of my life . To go away and meet new women and have a good time in the States . It all helped me tremendously .

The natural transistion from stubbies is to go to C-Legs ; they're a little heavier and a slightly different skill set to stubbies . I didn't know what the fuss was about , and when talking to the Major I was like ' Fuck it , just give me these stubbies , I'll walk around in them for the next 50 years ' . I just wanted to walk , finish my rehab , and get on with my life . But he persevered , and I'm glad he did . On stubbies you're basically like a Lada , where you can feel every bump on the road , and on C-Legs they're super charged legs with suspension and 4 wheel drive . Well , not quite , but you get the idea . Walking on C-Legs is like if you can imagine walking down a sandy dune and your feet are sinking into the sand as you descend . It's very similar in feeling . Enjoyable , but hard work .

MY FUTURE

I feel a whole lot better about the situation . For 6 months I was in a hazy cloud . Fighting back every day to regain some sort of feeling of which I once was . I drank a lot . It helped . Until I woke up one day and felt ill for the amount I was drinking . Within 2 weeks I was dry and feeling more myself . It was completely physical . What I lost on the battlefield I accepted . For real . I was hit that hard it took me 6 months to fully recover and feel myself .

When it became clear that I could no longer contribute to the Army , I wanted to forget about it and move on with my life . Forget about the Irish Guards . If I couldn't be part of it in a positive way , like before the incident , I just wanted to make a clean break . The Irish Guards were fantastic . They knew my personality , kept me in the loop , kept me involved , tortured me , wouldn't leave me alone . And I'm glad they did . Their supports been next to none .

When I leave Headley Court within the next year my intentions are to go back to education and possibly get a Degree in Geography . I love Geography . I think it's magical , and it's all around us . I would like to teach . Maybe it's the narcissist in me that wants to stand in front of an audience and perform ; or maybe it's just the opportunity to contribute , get involved and influence while helping people achieve their goals . I prefer that reason . I need to do something I'm only 27 . Educating myself will be easier this time around . I have fewer distractions and the loss of limbs has settled me down , a bit . I'm less likely to be confrontational as I'm not as capable and I guess people see me for a wounded soldier and tend to give me a bit of a wide birth . In many ways it's been a liberating experience . The accident as rendered me almost obsolete from a physical point of view compared to what I could do before . It's time to see what my cerebral powers are up to .

A degree isn't an overnight process and should grasp my full attention for a couple of years . That , and being the best example to my son George sit at the forefront of my mind . But I will always remember my short army career with the Irish Guards . I really have fought and dined with fine people . There's a mnemonic in the army SOLIDC , Selfless commitment , respect for Others , Loyalty , Integrity , Discipline and Courage . Some people preach it , I lived it . I'm not the same bloke I was rocking up from the streets of Belfast and I'm positively better for the experience . I have no regrets but the army is not something you can shake off you so easily . Everything reminds me of it . When I'm driving down the motorway with the window open it reminds me of the day that Chinook came in to rescue me and bring me back to Bastion . Although Tracey Chapman wasn't playing in the background in Afghan . When I see someone running a little voice inside me says ' keep going , keep her lit ' , the encouragement I would of saved for the boys in Battalion . It's over but I'll survive .

THE DAIRIES

When hit in Afghanistan there's a void from that point til you wake up . Some people are kept under for up to 2 weeks because of their injuries being so sever , like poor Manneh . He was kept under 2 weeks . I was 2 days . I responded well . I have vague memories when unbeknowingly I was in the ICU in Birmingham . A jock guy he'd been under for a week . He was screaming in an irate Glaswegian accent . They'd just woke him up . *' I fuckin' know I'm in Afghanistan , Don't you fuckin' lie to me '* . Continued for half an hour . It was frantic and piercing . To put it nicely I wished he'd be quiet .

In the ICU I imagined I was in a fish tank , bubbles were coming off the top of my curtain rails that surrounded my bed . Like , in a fish tank .

I also imagined that a Taliban commander had flew in by Heli and the Heli drop was 20m in front of my hospital bed through a set of double doors . I could hear and feel the heli land and then , take off . The doors blasted open . The Taliban commander started reading the riot act to the nurses and anyone in sight . He had a maroon beret , was about 5ft 6 wiry build with black beard and movie star looks . At the time it was so real . Isn't morphine a wonderful thing .

So the time were you lose consciousness and fully come round is sketchy and surreal .

These 2 books , more like little dairies , were threw on my bed 9 days into my recovery by an MLO . Some of what was written was very touching and meant a lot to me at the time . I was still very raw from the incident at the time .

Quote from 1984 taken from The Complete Works of George Orwell edited by Peter Davison , Published by Chat & Windus courtesy the estate of the late Sonia Brownell Orwell and used by permission of The Random House Group Limited .

F Med 1047

PATIENTS' DIARY

Intensive Care

Op _____

Name COLUM Mc GEOUGH

Rank CPSM

Admitted 2.2.10

Date & Time	Narrative	Signature
02 Feb 11	COLUM,	P HUNTER
	I WAS A MEMBER OF THE MERT	(HAZ)
	THAT CAME TO GET YOU. I	SAC
	CAME OUT INTO THE FIELD	PARAMEDIC
	TO TAKE THE HANDOVER	MERT
	FROM YOUR FRIENDS/MEDICS.	
	THEY HAD LOOKED AFTER YOU	
	WELL. WE BROUGHT YOU ONTO	
	THE CHINOOK, WE HAD TO PUT	
	A PAINFUL NEEDLE INTO YOUR	
	SHOULDER TO PUT YOU OFF	
	TO SLEEP AND THEN TO REPLACE	
	THE BLOOD YOU HAD LOST. IT	
	WAS MY HAND YOU HELD AS	
	YOU WENT OFF TO SLEEP.	
	WE CHECKED YOU FOR ANYTHING	
	THAT HAD MISSED ON THE	
	GROUND (NOTHING! - BRILLIANT!)	
	AFTER A VERY FAST FLIGHT	
	TO BASTION WE HANDED YOU	
	TO THE ER TEAM.	
2 FEB 11	COLUM,	KARI MARTIN
0930	I WAS PART OF THE	LCDR, RN
	TRAUMA TEAM OF BRITS	UNITED STATES
	AND AMERICANS THAT	NAVY
	CARED FOR YOU IN THE	
	EMERGENCY DEPARTMENT.	
	IT WAS HERE THAT WE	
	CONTROLLED YOUR BLEEDING,	

Date & Time	Narrative	Signature
	CONTINUED GIVING YOU BLOOD AND TOOK A PICTURE OF YOUR BODY WITH A CAT SCAN. WE ALL AGREED THAT YOU WERE VERY STRONG (OR "FIT" AS YOU BRITS SAY!) BECAUSE YOU WERE RESPONDING VERY WELL TO TREATMENT DESPITE YOUR INJURIES. AFTER STABILIZING YOU, WE TRANSFERRED YOU TO THE OPERATING ROOM. WE ARE ALL SO PROUD OF YOU, COLUM. SO VERY, VERY PROUD OF YOU FOR PUTTING YOUR LIFE ON THE LINE FOR US. GODSPEED STRONG BOY!	
02/02/11	Hey McGeown mate. I was Here when you flew into Bastion. The lads Done a great Job on you as the Ground. they have sent All there Best to you a said well all catch up	Adam Savage No2 Company

Date & Time	Narrative	Signature
02.2.11	WELL, WELL, WELL — BONKERS BOBBY MAGOO! I HOPE YOU'RE PAX'D UP MATE OTHERWISE I'M GOING TO BE RUNNING MARATHONS FOR THE REST OF MY LIFE TO KEEP YOU IN COWBOY HATS AND THAT HOUSE IN SCOTLAND — OR WAS IT SPAIN? IF THERE IS ONE PERSON CRAZY ENOUGH NOT TO LET THIS KNOCK THEM SIDEWAYS IT'' YOU I'LL LET BUTLER KNOW AS SOON AS YOUR MINIMISE GET'' LIFTED — ENJOY BIRMINGHAM AND I'LL MEET YOU THERE WHEN I GET BACK	BOB
02-2-11	YOUNG MAC. WHAT CAN I SAY. GUTTED, BUT ALSO LIKE YOU CAN TURN THIS AROUND. NURSES+ DOCTORS ARE DOING A GREAT JOB FOR YOU. KEEP STRONG AND I'LL SEE YOU IN A COUPLE OF WEEKS	SIMMY ROMS

Date & Time	Narrative	Signature
2·2·11	Colum, sorry to see you this way, but the staff are outstanding here, and in the UK. will see you in a few weeks as	Cecil
	Colum, GET YOURSELF ON THE MEMO AS SOON AS POSSIBLE! ME, JARVIS + KELLEHER NEED TO TAKE YOU OUT FOR A PINT YOU WAR HERO! Q.S.	Amos
2 Feb 11 16:30hrs LOCAL	Colum, It is the Rmo here just visiting you before your flight home to Birmingham for further care. Everyone has worked hard out here and I will continue to work hard for you as the Rmo when you get out of hospital and I get back to Windsor. Get well Quick! Rmo	MAJOR ▮▮▮ RAMC

Date & Time	Narrative	Signature
	With you when we get Back. Im Really sorry what happened to you your a good lad and am in oar off you. You've Done more than I could ever imaged get well soon mate Q.S	
2.2.11.	Colum. I'm one of the nurses that looked after you in ITU. I followed you all the way from the ambi - through into ITU. You had the best care possible mate from start to finish. The paramedics / RCRT did a good job. You sailed through ED and surgery. You probably won't remember anything we did for you as we made sure you slept using sm' Big Drugs - so no probs with your COT in a few weeks time. Take care and stay fit. I hope to hear your name in the Para olympics. Get well and work hard.	I. HAZZARD Player

Date & Time	Narrative	Signature
2.2.2011	I didn't expect to see you again so quickly Colin ... I have said prayers for you ~ again you at blessing and anointed you with Holy Oil. God grant you and your family strength in the time to come. I'll look forward to seeing you when we get back and help you in my prayers with Alex.	PADRE
2-2-2011	I am one of the surgeons that operated on you. We all here wish you the best and the best and quickest recovery	Di Russo
02.02.11	Colum, I know this wont slow you down much. Hopefully I'll see you when we get back, take care Uncle. QS Dave Kelleher.	

Date & Time	Narrative	Signature
2/2/11	Col it's oic you done fab once again you show us How it is to soilder on you'll be back to you old self in no time and guess what you can take you dog for a walk what you've been missing once you get back on your feet Sleep tight bro Little George will be waiting for you to land	
02Feb11	John McGeown, I am sorry to see you under these circumstance. Despite it being the early stages the medical staff are really happy with the progress you are making. Take care and good luck with your recovery and I'll see you when we are all back.	Capt Adjutant
02 feb 11	John McGeown, I'm extremely sorry to see you wounded and I'm frankly in	

Date & Time	Narrative	Signature
	awe of what you've done out on the ground I wish you all the best as you start your recovery; you have recieved the best possible treatment here. We'll miss you – but see you soon in Windsor. Quis Separabit	MAJ BN 2IC
2/2/11	Gdsm McGeown, I wish you all the best and a speedy recovery. I hope you are up and about! – No Time 1 I am extremely proud to have looked after No 2 Coy IG. From a Jock to a mick you can't keep the Celts down	Maj Vereas Gr' SSCOT
2/2/11	GDSM McGEOWN, I HOpe you have a speedy recovery mate and I am proud to have served with brave young soldiers like you – god speed	J Howe QM(T) 5 SCOTS

271

Date & Time	Narrative	Signature
2/2/11	Young Magowan Your a hero son keep the chin up and be good	Scott RQMS 5 SCOTS
2.2.11	Hi, I was one of the nurses on ITa at Camp Bastion, I hope you are making a good recovery all the best for the future	Stephen RAM RGN
	Hi McGowan mate Just a quick one from everyone in FOB KSR, the CQ and CSM wish you a speedy recovery and will catch up for a few Guinesses. Sorry about spelling mate Im a thick Scotsman, all the best See you in a couple of weeks Q.S. God speed my freind.	from CQ, CSM, 4plt 5plt, 6plt CQ SM savage

Date & Time	Narrative	Signature
3/2/11	GDSM McGEOWN, MY NAME IS LAURA, I AM AN RAF NURSE AND WAS PART OF THE 7 MAN 'CCAST' MISSION WHO PICKED YOU UP FROM KAF AND FLEW YOU BACK TO BIRMINGHAM. FROM ALL OF US ON THE TEAM TODAY WE WISH YOU ALL THE BEST FOR YOUR RECOVERY. BEST WISHES	L. GREAVES SGT RAF CCAST.
04/02/11 07:00	Hi Colum! I'm Mylene, one of the nurses here in Q.E.H, your back now in Birmingham I looked after you tonight. You're doing well after your surgery. We plan to wake you up this AM. All the best!	MYLENE PEOSO

Date & Time	Narrative	Signature
2 FEB 11	Hope all goes well for the next phase of your recovery, look forward to seeing you in Windsor. GS	OWT.
2 FEB 11	Stay strong and get well rocket, will see you back in Windsor	RQMS.
2/Feb 11	They Brushed your Teeth for you 101 god speed Mate See you soon	Grinch
2/FEB/11	GET STUCK INTO your recovery mucker and stay strong, Good luck and see you soon. All the Best	CQMS 4.
02/FEB/11	HELLO MATE, MY NAME IS PAUL, I'M ONE OF THE NURSES THAT LOOKED AFTER YOU IN BASTION ITU. WISHING YOU ALL THE BEST AND A SPEEDY RECOVERY. TAKE CARE	P. HALLAM (STAFF NURSE

THE GLOSSARY

FOB – Forward Operating base

PB – Patrol Base

G-man – Guardsman

Bluey – Military letter

HLS – Heli Landing Site

Multiple – Multiple of men

Andytown – Andersonstown/West Belfast

PSNI – Police Service Northern Ireland

RUC – Royal Ulster Constabulary

GAA – Gaelic Athletic Assosciation

The Road – Andersonstown Road

IC – In Command

Sally Ann – Salvation Army

Paisleyite - a pastor reminiscent in image and voice to the Reverend Ian Paisley .

DS – Directing Staff

CROW – Combat Recruit Of War

Swabbing – Cleaning

Beasting – To be pushed physically hard

Norgi – A huge olive green flask container that holds range stew or brew for the boys

PAX – What we call civilians on the ground

SOP – Standard Operating Procedure

PRR – Personal Radio

OT – Occupational Therapist

Phis – Physical training

' What was said '

" What I was thinking "

' *Negative or slang comment* '